Skiing and Sleeping on the Summits

Cascade Volcanoes of the Pacific Northwest

Skiing 20 Peaks in 30 Days

Jon Kedrowski, PhD

The Colorado Mountain Club Press
Golden, Colorado

Skiing & Sleeping on the Summits:
Cascade Volcanoes of the Pacific Northwest
Copyright © 2016 by Dr. Jon Kedrowski

PUBLISHED BY
The Colorado Mountain Club Press
710 Tenth Street, Suite 200, Golden, Colorado 80401
303-996-2743 e-mail: cmcpress@cmc.org

CONTACTING THE PUBLISHER
We would appreciate it if readers would alert us to any errors
or outdated information by contacting us at the address above.

DISTRIBUTED TO THE BOOK TRADE BY
Mountaineers Books, 1001 SW Klickitat Way, Suite 201
Seattle, WA 98134, 800-553-4453,
www.mountaineersbooks.org

The overview and chapter opening maps in this book were created using ArcGIS®
software by Esri. ArcGIS® and ArcMap™ are the intellectual property of Esri and are
used herein under license. Copyright © Esri. All rights reserved. For more information
about Esri® software, please visit www.esri.com. Redistribution rights are granted
by the data vendor for hardcopy renditions or static, electronic map images
(for example, .gif, .jpeg) that are plotted, printed, or publicly displayed with proper
metadata and source/copyright attribution to the respective data vendor/vendors.
Public domain data from the U.S. government is freely redistributable with proper
metadata and source attribution. ESRI, DigitalGlobe, GeoEye, i-cubed World Imagery
supplied December 2015. Maps produced by Sarah Jenniges

All summit specific topographic maps were
created using CalTopo software (caltopo.com).

We gratefully acknowledge the financial support of the
people of Colorado through the Scientific and Cultural Facilities
District of greater Denver for our publishing activities.

Cover and text design by Rebecca Finkel, F + P Graphic Design

First Edition
ISBN: 978-1-937052-35-5
Printed in China

PLEASE NOTE: Risk is always a factor in backcountry and high mountain travel.
Many of the activities described in this book can be dangerous, especially when
weather is adverse or unpredictable, and when unforeseen events or conditions
create a hazardous situation. The author has done his best to provide the reader
with accurate information, as well as point out some potential hazards. It is the
responsibility of the reader to learn the necessary skills for safe travel, and to
exercise caution in potentially hazardous areas. The author and publisher disclaim
any liability for injury or other damage caused by mountain travel, skiing, or
performing any other activity described in this book.

In addition, people are responsible for knowing and obeying local agency rules
and regulations. Many U.S. National Parks and federal lands require permits to
camp overnight and some require camping in designated sites or areas only.
Please check for any trail or route closures and adhere to posted signs indicating
closures or restrictions. Use the backcountry safely and responsibly to enhance
your backcountry experience. Adhere to the "Leave No Trace" principles
and ethics to help minimize impact.

I dedicate this adventure
in memory of my grandmother,
Leona M. Kedrowski

Contents

"The journey to climb, ski, and overnight on 20 Cascade volcanoes in 30 days began as all do—with an idea. An inconsequential, ethereal thought, a suggestion that gradually built momentum into a tangible entity with a force of its own to sweep one along until it becomes reality.

But perhaps we are getting ahead of ourselves. The idea was actually spawned several years ago, concocted in the mind of a son of Vail, who outgrew the big, 14,000-foot mountains of his native state of Colorado after climbing them all in high school, then again in a span of forty days despite a two-week interlude in Russia, and yet again with an overnight bag strapped to his back, sleeping at their apexes and telling the story in Sleeping On The Summits: Colorado Fourteener High Bivys. Kudos to Dr. Jon for continuing his story on the Ring of Fire. Skiing and Sleeping on the Summits is truly taking the Cascade volcanoes to the next level."

—MIKE LEWIS

Director of Brand Activation and Digital Strategy, Zeal Optics

"What Dr. Jon has done by skiing the highest volcanoes in the Pacific Northwest and camping on their summits is nothing short of extraordinary. His project is yet another example of how we can all 'strive for greatness' by having a true N.O.D. (No Off Days) mentality."

—BOB PIETRACK

Head Men's Basketball Coach, Fort Lewis College

"The beauty of the Cascade Volcanoes is rivaled only by their scale. Climbing any of these giants of the Lower 48 is a huge achievement for any mountaineer, and Jon Kedrowski managed to capture the experience and chronicled it wonderfully in his new book, Skiing and Sleeping on the Summits: Cascade Volcanoes of the Pacific Northwest."

—TED MAHON

Photographer and ski mountaineer

Summit of Broken Top, with views clear across the Cascade Volcanoes in Northern Oregon.

SILVER OAK

salutes Dr. Jon Kedrowski's incredible story
of *Skiing and Sleeping on the Summits:
Cascade Volcanoes of the Pacific Northwest.*

Dr. Jon begins his journey to climb and ski the 20 highest volcanoes in
the Pacific Northwest atop Mount Shasta (14,179'), and skis each peak
including Diamond Peak with a bottle of Silver Oak close at hand.

The Duncan Family of Silver Oak and Twomey proudly congratulates Dr. Jon Kedrowski. Across his travels and adventures, Dr. Kedrowski has carried the Silver Oak bottle high atop the Volcanoes of Northern California and the entire Pacific Northwest.

Jon with Silver Oak President & CEO David Duncan atop Bald Mountain, (12,200') near Vail, CO.

Jon with CMC Board President Kevin Duncan on the summit of Turret Peak (13,835').

Raymond Twomey Duncan (1930-2015)
This book is also dedicated to the memory of Raymond T. Duncan, the wine pioneer of Silver Oak. A true skier and alpine explorer, he was the founder of Purgatory Ski resort near Durango Colorado in 1965, former chairman of the board for Colorado Ski Country USA. Inducted into the Colorado Ski and Snowboard Hall of Fame in 2006.

Skiing 20 peaks in 30 days: that is
impressive. I definitely commend
his commitment. It's a daunting task:
walking early, packing enough food,
dealing with weather, keeping focused
and healthy. To do that many in
30 days can be the toughest thing
anyone will do in their life; and to do
it as a lone wolf at times, out there
like Jon, that makes it even harder.

—CHRIS DAVENPORT
The legendary Old Snowmass Red Bull athlete
led a team of skiers up and down 15 Pacific
Northwest Volcanoes in 14 days in 2012.

Chris Davenport on the summit of Mount Hood, May 13, 2012, during his Ring of Fire Volcano Tour. Mount Jefferson, which he skied the day prior, can be seen out in the distance to the south. Photo by Ted Mahon

"Visible from hundreds of miles away, the enormous relief of the Cascade Volcanoes beckons skier mountaineers. Their summits are hard-earned, but the reward is worth the effort, offering some of the longest ski lines and the largest vertical that a ski mountaineer might ever get to experience."

—TED MAHON
Photographer and Ski Mountaineer

Foreword

W elcome to Sneffels," is all I heard. It was July, 2011. I immediately straightened up in my sleeping bag to see what was going on. I saw a dark silhouette that looked like Frankenstein, and as it turned out, that silhouette was Jon. I looked at my watch and it read 4:00 a.m. Jon had uttered his version of a formal greeting for two delirious climbers approaching the 14,150-foot summit of Mount Sneffels with their headlamps beaming under a starry sky. The climbers had pulled an all-nighter to reach the summit to catch the sunrise. To us it was old hat. We broke old rules and blazed a new approach to mountaineering in Colorado.

I've never been a part of anything that taught me so much so quickly. I witnessed the growth and decay of thunderstorms from 14,000 feet, and in the process discovered a chasm that exists between modeled orographic convection and reality. *Sleeping on the Summits: Colorado Fourteener High Bivys* will never be repeated on such a short timeline. Jon rolled the dice. He learned as we went along. He adapted and persevered. It remains one of the very best examples of teamwork in my life.

Fast-forward to May, 2014, and "Welcome to Rainier" is all I heard. The dream continued this time high atop the Ring of Fire. Magma swirled beneath the Earth's crust just feet from some of Jon's summit camps. My phone buzzed at all hours in search of weather forecasts. I remember going to bed thinking about Shasta, Lassen, Glacier, Hood, and of course, Adams and Rainier.

Jon's success in both projects is often linked to our friendship and teamwork, as well as his ability to go all out past anything anyone would consider within the norm. It's proof that anything is possible if you surround yourself with the best people and are willing to take calculated risks. Welcome to *Skiing and Sleeping on the Summits: Cascade Volcanoes of the Pacific Northwest.* Strap on your skis and get ready; you are in for an exciting ride! *See you on the summit!*

—CHRIS TOMER, Meteorologist

"Jon took the successful lessons of *Sleeping on the Summits: Colorado Fourteener High Bivys* and applied them to the Ring of Fire."   —CHRIS TOMER

Full moon setting on the summit of Mount Adams, casting a gorgeous shadow with Mount Saint Helens and Mount Rainier in the distance as the sun rises.

Crevasses on Mount Rainier, with Mount Adams in the distance.

Icons of West Coast Identity: Cascade Volcanoes

Mount Rainier is arguably the most recognizable icon and mountaineering goal of the Lower Forty-Eight for any aspiring alpinist. At 14,410 feet, it is visible from the nearby metropolis of Seattle and dominates the landscape of the Pacific Northwest. It sees about 10,000 aspiring climbers per year, all with different reasons for why they climb. In 2010, I tried to answer the "Why Climb" question, and based my Doctoral Dissertation on climber perceptions of hazards and risks while mountaineering. I also looked at the permit system management of Mount Rainier. I have been doing research on peaks in the Pacific Northwest, Alaska, and California ever since I first climbed Mount Rainier in 2008.

But Mount Rainier isn't the only significant volcano along the North American West Coast. In the spring of 2014, I spent significant time and effort to accomplish yet another first in my climbing and ski-mountaineering career. I traveled up the West Coast starting with

Mount Shasta in California May 1st and finished with Mount Baker in Washington on May 31st. I climbed and skied 250 miles covering over 100,000 vertical feet for the twenty highest Cascade volcanoes in thirty days, and also spent the night on some of the most iconic summits of the Pacific Northwest, including peaks like Mount Hood, South Sister, Mount Thielsen, Mount Adams, and Mount Rainier.

The Ring of Fire and the Cascade Volcanic Arc

While Mounts Rainier, Hood, and St. Helens get the majority of the press these days (most commonly for climbing accidents or geologic activity) and are most visited by hikers and alpinists, there are more than twenty-five other high volcanoes comprising the Cascade Volcanic Arc stretching from Northern California to Oregon and into northern Washington. Lesser volcanoes such as Mount Washington and Three-Fingered Jack are also located in Oregon, but aren't included in this book. (Mount Bailey, at 8,376', was also attempted on this trip, but due to extremely bad weather, and lack of visibility, the peak wasn't summitted but only partly skied, and hence I decided not to include it in this book.) However, the entire Cascade Volcanic Arc bordering the Pacific Ocean along the West Coast is part of the Pacific Ring of Fire. These volcanoes are here because of the subduction of the oceanic Juan de Fuca Plate under the North American Plate. The Juan de Fuca Plate is a smaller separate tectonic plate located on the ocean bottom and is just to the east of the larger Pacific Plate. Convergence between the Juan de Fuca Plate and the North American Plate continues at a rate of about 4 to 5 centimeters (1.6 to 2 inches) per year. The convergence and subduction zone has created the disruption of subsurface crust of the earth along the coastal mountains of the Pacific Northwest. Magma below the surface has been pushed near the top of these mountains to create not only instability, but in many locations steam vents, sulfuric gasses, and lahars (landslides of wet volcanic debris) that have permanently marked the landscape. From these processes, the Cascade Range has been volcanically active for about 36 million years, and some rocks on the volcanoes range from 42 to 55 million years old.

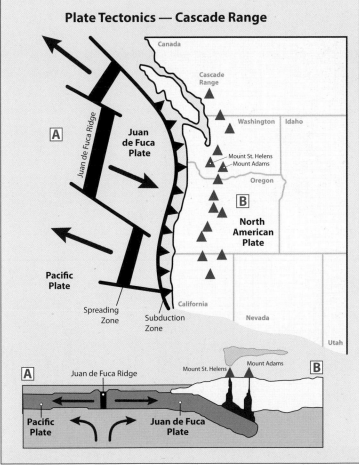

Types of Volcanoes

The formation of the great volcanoes of the Cascade Volcanic Arc was caused by plate tectonics along the Pacific Ring of Fire, as mentioned in the previous section. From this tectonic activity along the West Coast, the most common volcanoes in this book are the composite cones known as stratovolcanoes. Nevertheless, there are four major types of volcanoes found globally and during this ski odyssey:

1. Shield

When numerous successive basaltic lava flows occur in a given region, they pile up into a shape of a large and very long concave mountain, often resembling a knight's shield. The gently sloping, domed-shaped cones of Hawaii's volcanoes (Mauna Loa is the largest on earth) are the best example. In this book, Diamond Peak in Oregon is perhaps the best shield volcano example in the Pacific Northwest. Shield volcano eruptions involve long periods of flowing lava and are not very explosive.

2. Cinder Cone

The smallest type of volcano, typically only a few hundred meters high. These volcanoes generally consist of large gravel-sized pyroclastics formed from a central vent but related to a nearby or collapsed composite cone volcano. The best examples of cinder cones in this book include Wizard Island in Crater Lake National Park, Oregon, or the many small cinder cone volcanoes within Lassen Volcanic National Park, California.

3. Composite Cone (Stratovolcano)

The most common type of volcano; some eruptions are effusive, while others are explosive. Famous examples of these stratovolcanoes include Mounts Rainier, Adams, Hood, Shasta, and Three Sisters. These volcanoes are constructed by layers (strata) of pyroclastics and lava. The composite cone is your classic volcano shape—slopes are gentle at the base and much steeper near the top. Unerupted andesite rock can also clog up the main and peripheral vents to these volcanoes, and over time this pressure can be released in the form of poisonous gasses and explosive pyroclastic eruptions, producing major destructive landslides, lahars, and debris flows.

4. Plug Dome

These volcanoes are formed when extremely viscous silica-rich magma pushes its way toward the surface of a volcanic cone's central vent but blocks the exit to the volcano. Over time a dome-shaped summit is formed. Sometimes jagged blocks from the pressure of the volcano are created near the summits and on the steep slopes of these peaks. The best example of a plug dome in this book is the Lassen Peak volcano in California. The potential for extremely explosive eruptions are characteristic of a plug dome volcano as the pressure on these plugs and steep slopes produces a powerful eruption.

Occasionally, the eruption of any one of these four types of volcanoes expels so much material and relieves so much pressure within the magma chamber that only a large and deep depression remains in the area that previously contained the volcano's summit. A large depression made in this way is termed a caldera. The best known caldera in North America and in this book is Crater Lake, formed by the eruption and subsequent collapse of Mount Mazama thousands of years ago.

Summit of Mount Hood, Mother's Day, 2012. The plan was to ski the Cooper Spur which faces northeast, and since the summit was reached quite early the skiers in Chris Davenport and Ted Mahon's "Ring of Fire Team" had to wait for the sun to warm and soften the snow. Photo by Ted Mahon

Sleeping on the Summit of a Cascade Volcano (and Skiing Down!)

Essentials to Consider

This tour of the Cascade volcanoes showcases sleeping on summits as well as skiing many classic routes on the volcanoes, yet this book is by no means an exhaustive guide.

In the sections of this book that discuss the ski descents and potential ski lines, as well as "Dr. Jon's Recommendations," here are how those routes are classified:

Easy Slopes ● Terrain that includes wide-open snow slopes, minimal crevassed terrain on glaciers, and steepness less than 25 degrees. This also includes logging roads, access roads, or Snowcat roads. Avalanche Danger Low.

Intermediate ■ Terrain that includes wide couloirs, minor gullies, moderately crevassed terrain on glaciers, and steepness between 25 and 35 degrees. This also includes hillsides that have dispersed trees, glades, or moderately forested terrain. Avalanche Danger Moderate.

Expert/Advanced ◆ Terrain that includes couloirs, gullies, heavily crevassed terrain on glaciers, and steepness between 35 and 50 degrees. This also includes hillsides with complex terrain and thicker forests. Avalanche Danger can be High.

Expert/Extreme ◆◆ Terrain that includes steep narrow couloirs, deep gullies, cornices, extremely crevassed terrain on glaciers, and steepness greater than 50 degrees. Cliffs and the ability to ski off of cliffs and cornices may be mandatory, as well as the ability to rappel down sections if necessary. Tree skiing and vegetation in forests may be very steep, thick, and extremely difficult to navigate and ski. Avalanche Danger can be Extreme.

Mount Thielsen

Do you want to sleep on the top of a Cascade Volcano?

Here's what I learned after sleeping on most and skiing from the top of many:

The most important variable to consider is the weather. Before packing a single bag, be sure you understand the weather forecast inside and out. Equally as important, educate yourself on mountain meteorology. Being able to diagnose the weather you see unfolding in the field can save your life. This kind of wisdom will help you decide whether to attack the summit or turn around and go home. Consult local weather experts for information, or attend personalized mountain meteorology workshops.

Know the mountain geography, specifically the route topography. Research the peak and know the escape routes if bad weather rolls in. Know where the last possible water stops are to lighten your load. Knowing the route will also give you a good estimate of how long it will take you to reach the summit. Keep in mind you'll be carrying overnight gear and will only be as fast as your heaviest pack and slowest group member. Understanding topography can also help you select the route safest from avalanche danger.

Increase your fitness and acclimatization ahead of time. Efficiency is a key piece of the puzzle, and if you're in great shape you can move faster and feel better. Sleep on a 9,000- or 10,000-foot volcano first, then increase the elevation gradually to experiences on 12ers or 13ers to further acclimatize. If a dangerous storm moves in you'll want to have the stamina, speed, and fitness to escape.

Lighten your load. The more weight you carry, the slower you will move. Heavy weight also increases fatigue. I was a bare-minimalist during this project, so you'll have to experiment to see what you can survive without. I found the essentials to be my whippet/ice axe, a 15-degree down ultralight sleeping bag, a sleeping pad, an ultralight one-person tent, an ultralight bivy sack, an ultralight hoody down jacket, rain jacket and rain pants, water reservoir, headlamp, energy bars, hat, gloves, cameras, sunscreen, sunglasses, toilet paper, ultraviolet water purifier, and pre-packed pizza. Most of the time I didn't bring a stove. Hot food and hot beverages are luxuries, but may also be essential at times, especially on frozen volcanoes. On a few of the multi-day peaks and glaciated volcanoes, I carried a stove, but it was a very small and light MSR Pocket-Rocket. In avalanche terrain, a beacon, probe, and shovel are essential, but remember that they won't prevent you from being caught in an avalanche, they will only help you find and dig others out. A beacon will also facilitate your own rescue, should you be caught in an avalanche. My ski equipment consisted of the Kastle TX 177 and 187 touring line with Dynafit bindings and Scarpa Maestrale touring boots.

Know your limits. You'll want to climb the Cascade volcanoes in traditional alpine style before attempting an overnight bivy. Realize that you will be skiing or snowboarding down a peak with a heavy pack, and that makes even moderate terrain that much more difficult and dangerous. Learn to ski difficult terrain, and how to assess avalanche conditions in the field. Before you leave on a ski trip, browse websites for avalanche information and reports. Start easy and build from there. After having led numerous groups up 14ers and volcanoes, including Mount Rainier, I've found that it's often one of the most difficult things these hikers or skiers have ever done.

Meteorology: Regional Weather and Climate

In an average winter, the Pacific Northwest receives anywhere from 400 to 1,100 inches of snow per year. Most of the snow falls between November and May in the higher elevations and on the volcanoes. Generally, in May, the change of seasons produces high pressure that can settle over inland areas of Northern California, Oregon, and Washington. In spring, the high pressure can settle in for days, providing warm, stable weather, which becomes more prolonged by summer's arrival in late June. Because the seasons are changing, socked-in periods of rain also occur, when it can still rain and snow for days at a time. At lower elevations, the distinct mesothermal marine West Coast climate and maritime influence lends itself to the temperate rain forest with thick and lush vegetation. But don't be fooled by the stable weather of the summer months and relatively mild winters in this part of the North American continent. Higher elevations not only receive the lion's share of the seasonal snowfall, but they also experience heavy downpours of rain and can experience intense blizzards and strong winds at any time of the year.

The orographic (rain shadow) effect also plays a significant role in weather and highland climate of the Pacific Northwest. Snowfall and overall precipitation is generally less to the east of the Cascade Crest, and the eastern aspects of the volcanoes generally receive less precipitation than the windward cooler and wetter sides of the volcanoes. At the same time, this is precisely the reason why there is typically more snowfall on the more coastally located Mount Baker, versus Glacier Peak, or more snowfall is usually recorded on Mount Hood over Mount Thielsen. Even the Three Sisters can be hit with a bit more snow than Mount Bachelor because they are located farther to the north and west and catch the prevailing fronts off the Pacific Ocean. These general trends are important to keep in mind, especially in regards to understanding snowpack and avalanche potential with increasing elevation on the Cascade volcanoes.

Snow and Avalanches in the Pacific Northwest

The most unpredictable phenomenon related to weather forecasting and skiing on the Cascade volcanoes are avalanches. Most avalanches (up to 80 percent) are human triggered, and therefore nearly 100 percent preventable. However, the only way to prevent an avalanche is to not go out and enjoy skiing in the backcountry or venturing out to climb and ski the volcanoes in the first place. This is not realistic, of course, but there are many steps an educated and experienced backcountry skier and alpinist can take to decrease the chances of ever being caught in an avalanche.

Four Human Factors for Avalanche Avoidance

1. Become Experienced and Educated: Take avalanche courses, and if you have never been out climbing and skiing volcanoes before, go with someone who knows what they are doing. You can always learn something from others. Get out and explore as often as possible. You can learn a great deal from just being out on the peaks all the time.

2. **Terrain Selection and Good Route-finding Habits:** Carrying the proper equipment is important, but if you steer clear of extremely steep slopes, avoid overhanging cornices, and stay away from glaciers that are heavily crevassed, you can minimize your risk. Proper backcountry travel is a skill that is learned over many years. Always consider what is above you when climbing, think often about your escape route, and never linger in an area that might be prone to avalanches. Travel through high-risk areas one at a time, and try to stay above and cross potential avalanche paths as high as possible.

3. **Never Go Out Alone:** I approach this one with discretion—about 60 percent of my adventures are done solo as I enjoy solitude. Going solo is a matter of preference, but can be very rewarding for the experienced alpinist. The rewards can also be great if you have an equal partner because you can learn a great deal from one another in the mountains.

4. **Start Early:** Many mistakes in the backcountry are created and compounded from other mistakes. The root of the problem is often not starting early enough and running out of time, which makes us rush and make rash decisions leading to mistakes and accidents. For example, in April, May, and June, the Pacific Northwest snowpack is generally more predictable and stable compared to winter months. Snow heats up and softens in the afternoons from warmer temperatures and direct sunlight. The snowpack settles, freezes, and stabilizes overnight when it gets cold. It is generally a good rule to begin an ascent in safe, frozen, and stable snow well before dawn, to be on the summit at sunrise or at least before 9:00 a.m. on a very warm day, and to be skiing down a steep slope or narrow couloir when the snow becomes corn—when it is soft enough to ski but not soft enough to create a wet slab avalanche. Powder days are in a different category, but starting early is still a good rule so that you are down and out of harm's way before noon.

The Avalanche Triangle

The human factors mentioned above can be placed within the "Avalanche Triangle," first described by Fesler and Fredston in *Snow Sense,* first published in 1984. The triangle has three sides: terrain, weather, and snowpack. Each will be briefly described here.

Snowpack   Terrain

Weather

A fourth variable, human actions, creates the avalanche hazard.
Photo by Ivan Larson

Terrain

The magical slope angle for avalanches is 35 degrees. This is the most important factor to consider whether or not a slide can occur. Slope aspect determines if sun exposure is hitting a slope indirectly or not. Slope aspect can also determine the impact of wind, which can load snow onto a slope. Overall, north-facing slopes tend to be more prone to avalanches because the snow is colder and slower to bond together. "Faceting," or crystallization of snow creating a weak layer, can also happen more on north-facing slopes. While slopes with northerly aspects (opposite in the southern hemisphere with southerly aspects) remain cold, slopes with south-facing aspects often develop a sun crust that can act as a sliding layer. Moderate warming on a slope can stabilize the snowpack, but rapid warming, especially within a day's time or on very warm spring days from direct sunlight, can have the opposite effect and can cause avalanches.

Weather

Snowpack can be constantly changed by the weather. The best question to ask is, "How is the weather impacting the snow's strength?" Past, current, and future weather can dictate snowpack and the likelihood of avalanches. Digging a snow pit near a slope you want to ski is a good way to check snow layers for stability and to see what the weather was doing to the snowpack in the past months. Layers will have different densities or hardness showing periods of drought, heavy snowfall, or mild days and cold nights when depth hoar was created.

For current weather, understanding how it is impacting snow and conditions is critical. For example, is it snowing heavily or lightly, and for how long has it been snowing? How much snow has fallen, and is the temperature rising or falling? Quickly rising temperatures combined with sunlight can lead to snow settling and creeping downhill due to gravity.

Heavy snowfall that accumulates at an inch per hour, or twelve inches in less than twenty-four hours, can have a significant impact on snowpack and snow stability. The weight of the snow will be dictated by the moisture content and temperature. Colder snow is lighter and more powdery and can be less dangerous than warmer, wetter, and heavier snow. Wind plays a factor. If winds are stronger than 20 mph they can not only impact our visibility of route hazards, but can also transport snow to cornices and load it onto slopes, making them immediately more dangerous.

Knowing what future weather is forecasted is very helpful when planning a trip. I usually check the weather forecast to see what happened overnight and what is in store for the day. Red flags include more than six inches of new snow, high winds, more snow forecasted, and rapid warming for the day. Be aware that conditions may change as you get out into the backcountry or to a summit. Use general weather information to your advantage, but realize that "You never know until you go." I never cancel a trip because someone else told me to—I will still get out in the field and see for myself. If conditions indicate too many hazards, I can always pull the plug thirty minutes into the trip, but will have learned more from that experience than if I had stayed home.

Snowpack

To create a slab avalanche, the snowpack must have a slab, a weak layer, and a bed surface. What makes snow strong or weak, bonded or slippery, is mainly determined by how it changes when it hits the ground. The changes, also called snow metamorphism, either create strong internal cohesion through rounding, or create weak cohesion through faceting and crystallization. The latter results in unstable snowpack and "sugar" snow, which is heavily avalanche prone.

Volcanoes as Part of the Maritime Snowpack

In the Pacific Northwest, the volcanoes are considered maritime in their location. They are bordering the ocean, and generally the winters are mild without extreme cold, except at the highest elevations. The following avalanche characteristics are true of the maritime Cascade volcanoes:

1. Deep snowpack (more than 3 meters / 9 feet)

2. Warm temperatures (23 to 41 degrees Fahrenheit, -5 to 5 degrees Celsius)

3. High-density snow (10 to 20 percent water by volume)

4. Frequent storms with lots of snow

5. Weak layers are less pronounced and do not persist

6. Avalanches generally occurring during storms are triggered by precipitation or wind, as well as the human element

7. Midwinter rain common and can stabilize snowpack

8. Wet slides possible throughout the year, especially in the afternoon

There are some local variations in these trends in the Cascade volcanoes, dependent upon elevation and orographic effects, as well as latitude and distance from the Pacific Coast.

Good luck and be safe out there on your adventures!

Summit crater of South Sister.

The sun rises on a new adventure in the summit crater of Mount Rainier.

PREFACE

New Dreams, New Goals

What was I thinking? The sun was going down fast and it would be dark soon. I couldn't feel my fingers, and sub-zero winds were blasting me. "How could it be mid-August?" I asked myself. It was freezing! But I had to do it, had to put my tent directly on the summit of Washington's highest peak, the iconic volcano called Mount Rainier. The giant stratovolcano towers over the surrounding Cascade peaks, and my views stretched from the Snake River Valley in Idaho to the east, to the Pacific Ocean to the west. From this vantage point I could also see up into Canada and down into central Oregon.

My tent was barely anchored against the wind, but I was standing on the true summit of Mount Rainier, on the western flanks of the crater rim known as Columbia Crest. I had made up my mind that it would probably be best to place my tent directly on the summit, overlooking the crater. It was windy, yet this spot would be ideal for the magnificent vistas and handful of volcanoes that stretched north and south of me. It was mid-summer, 2011, and I was about thirty-five peaks into a crazy idea I called the Colorado Fourteener Bivys project. I was trying to become the first person to camp on the summit of the fifty-eight highest peaks in Colorado. So far so good, and since I was in Washington, I decided to try my luck on Mount Rainier as well.

Hours earlier in the calm winds and bright morning sunshine, I led three friends to the summit of Rainier. One of them was my former college professor, Chuck Schaefer, who invited me out every year to lead him and his daughters to the top of Rainier. The Schaefer bunch was always up for a good challenge on "The Mountain." It put a smile on my face knowing that just a few hours earlier I had been standing on this same spot with great friends. Chuck shed some tears that morning having made it to the top for a third time himself, but for the first time with both his daughters, Krista and Sonja, who were aged seventeen and twenty at the time. This is why I loved climbing and had made such a great career of it—the experiences were always special. I was committed to come back and spend the night, so I climbed back up from Ingraham Flats that evening for my second summit of the day.

The sun setting on the top of Mount Rainier on a very windy evening.

But on the summit that night I was battling major adversity, with the wind just about destroying my tent. I was left with two partially bent poles and a shelter that couldn't withstand the 50 mph gusts. Why was I even thinking about doing this again? A new summit and another overnight bivy, of course! Adventure, uncertainty, pain, suffering—it sounds enticing, right? Ha! Wrong. There has got to be a better way. The wind quickly dislodged some of the rocks and set my tent free. Oh, no! It was blown for 100 feet or so down into the broad and flat crater. My sleeping bag and tent fortunately became lodged and tangled in some nearby sun cups. The tent came to rest right side up and stopped tumbling. "Wait a minute, no wind down there!" So I grabbed my pack and relocated into the crater. "What a great campsite!"

Twenty minutes later I had bent the poles back into position, re-anchored my tent, got settled in, and was brewing up some hot drinks. The sunset was spectacular! Then I couldn't help but wonder—what about climbing the highest peaks in other states besides Colorado and across the globe? What about skiing these volcanoes in the Pacific Northwest and even spending the night on some of the summits? I could see at least six other volcanoes from the top of this one, and knew there were many more on the West Coast of the United States. Everyone is familiar with mountains like Rainier, Baker, and Hood in the Pacific Northwest, but what about the lesser-known volcanoes, peaks like Thielsen, McLoughlin, or Broken Top? "Ah, maybe in a few years," I thought and chuckled as I fell asleep to infinite possibilities.

— JON KEDROWSKI

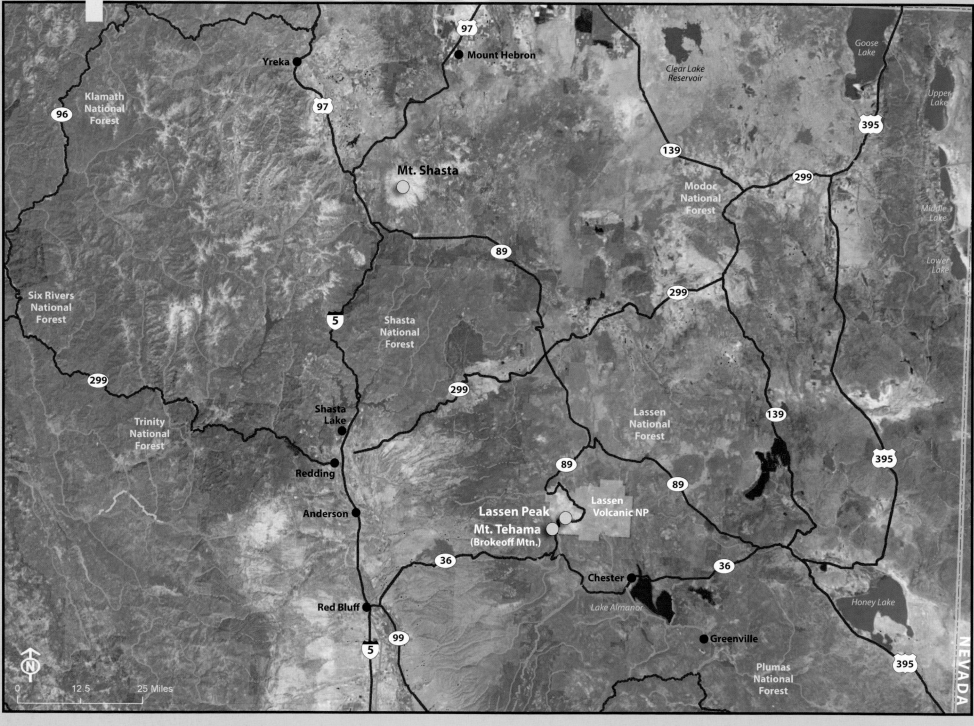

Mount Lassen painted by Lisa Martin

"A lot of times there's a reason you shouldn't be up on a mountain. When you're actually able to be up there, it feels like you're getting away with something. I am guilty of pushing the limits. Mountains are kind of like life, you get to suffer through strong winds and tough conditions, but it's worth the views and big lines you get to ski. But if you think skiing the volcanoes of the Pacific Northwest is difficult, then try skiing them and sleeping on their summits."   —JON KEDROWSKI

Mount Shasta

Mount Shasta

Mighty White Uytaahkoo

14,179 ft | 4,317 m (41° 24′ 33″ N; 122° 11′ 42″ W)
Bivy and Ski April 30–May 1, 2014
First Ascent E.D. Pierce, 1854
First Ski Descent Fletcher Hoyt et al., 1947

First Bivy and Ski

I hadn't spent the night above 14,000 feet for almost a year, so it felt great to be heading up toward the top of Shasta. I planned on easing my way into my new project, so I wanted to use the entire day to go up Shasta and set up camp atop the towering Northern California volcano. I had awakened that morning in a hotel room in the nearby town of Shasta, and decided to at least catch the sunrise by way of the Everett Memorial Highway en route to Bunny Flat and the start of my long slog up the Mighty White Mountain.

Loaded up with a heavy pack complete with overnight gear—my tent, sleeping bag, stove, and plenty of warm clothes, the summit looked far away. "Here we go again," I said to myself, as I felt the excruciating weight of the pack, making it difficult to clip into my skis, which I would use on this trip to skin toward the summit and then ski back down to my vehicle the next morning. It had been nearly two years since I had completed the feat in Colorado where I became the only person to sleep on each of the fifty-eight Colorado 14,000-foot peaks. It was great to be back with a new goal and a new plan. They say, "A goal without a plan is just a wish" (attributed to Antoine de Saint-Exupery), and this time I had my work cut out for me to reach my latest goal. One peak at a time, but I wanted to try and ski the twenty highest Cascade volcanoes entirely

At the summit camp saying farewell to the last rays of the day.

within the month of May. While I knew this mission was going to be lofty, I felt like it would be realistic, yet I didn't want to pressure myself into making bad decisions. I decided that on this entire trip I would climb as many peaks as possible, ski from every mountain that would let me, and also spend the nights on the summits of the peaks if the weather allowed.

The weather forecast for the next several days was favorable. I had studied some of the weather models the day before and even had a nice phone call from an old friend, meteorologist Chris Tomer, who—just like old times—was standing by in his weather center ready to send me updates like we had done so many times in the past. Dry weather was forecast with moderate winds, so I was anxious to see how that played out up high that day.

Skis pointed down into the summit crater, ready to drop over 7,000' vertical.
Overview: The sun about to set over the Pacific Ocean, barely visible from the top on a calm evening above 14,000'.

Climbing up one of the narrow couloirs of the Red Banks in the Heart of the Upper Avalanche Gulch.

Ski Descents and Potential Ski Lines

Mount Shasta may be considered the best Cascade volcano to learn on and carry out your backcountry ski-mountaineering missions. All levels of terrain are found on the different regions of the volcano. There are few crevasse hazards to contend with on the mountain's seven glaciers, and the peak's most popular approach from Bunny Flat is accessed by way of the Everitt Memorial Highway, which is plowed even in the winter. I was fortunate to ski directly off the summit, down Misery Hill and to the Avalanche Gulch Direct Chute, while enjoying 7,000 vertical feet back to my vehicle parked at Bunny Flat. Shasta boasts over a dozen amazing ski lines dropping off the summit from all directions. It is certainly possible in the right snow conditions and time of year to get up to 10,000 vertical feet on any side of the giant volcano. There are many more routes than described here to ski on Shasta, which probably has the most abundant ski potential in all of the Cascades.

Transitioning near Thumb Rock with full view down onto the Konwatkiton Glacier.

Dr. Jon's Recommendations

◆ **Avalanche Gulch** Round-trip distance is 11 miles and 7,300'. The ascent may take 6–12 hours and you can descend in 1–3 hours. This classic standard "John Muir" route is also the route of the first ski descent in 1947. From the summit descend southwest down Misery Hill and then there are a handful of choices to ski up to five or six different variations through the Red Banks and the Heart between 11,500 and 13,000 feet. Expect to see people as the Bunny Flat Trailhead accessed from the Everitt Memorial Highway is the most popular place on Mount Shasta to climb and ski.

◆◆/◆ **Casaval Ridge** The southwest ridge of Shasta is long and a great ski-mountaineering objective. There are many options to descend this route. You can choose a handful of steep 50–60-degree couloirs dropping southeast into Avalanche Gulch or southwest into Cascade Gulch.

◆ **Cascade Gulch, Hidden Valley Variation** This long west and southwest face of the mountain has a couple of very desirable lines that drop for up to 4,000 vertical feet. The actual Cascade Gulch route ascends to a saddle between Shastina and Shasta near the top of the Whitney Glacier, and the ridge offers protection from avalanche-prone faces of the Hidden Valley Variation in mid-winter.

■ ● **South Slopes** Gentle Blue/Green slopes below Lake Helen make for excellent sunny spring corn skiing. You have a choice of continuing back down the direction of the Sierra Club Hut and Sand Flat, or to the south to Bunny Flat. An outing from Bunny Flat Trailhead to just above Lake Helen can be an all-day affair, still giving you over 3,500 vertical feet of skiing.

◆ ■ **Wintum Ridge / Wintum Glacier** The steepest sections of the ridge are just below the flat and large summit area south of the Hotlum Cone. The Wintum Ridge descends east and the slope angle decreases as you drop in elevation. Watch for crevasses in late spring if you choose to travel or ski down onto the Wintum Glacier farther northeast in the direction of Ash Creek. Skiing southeast from the ridge at treeline at 9,500' will take you down into Cold Creek basin.

◆◆/◆ **Holtum-Wintum Chute / East Couloir.** This is a unique and seldom skied line direct off the top of the Hotlum Cone. There is a beautiful ski line down a broad couloir that takes you directly east and allows you to choose between the Hotlum–Wintum Ridge to skier's left (northeast), Hotlum Glacier (north), or the Wintum Glacier to skier's right (northeast) after your first thousand feet.

Dr Jon's Extra Credit: These other climbing routes can offer great ski descents, too: **Sargent's Ridge, Hotlum Glacier, Hotlum-Bolam Ridge, Bolam Glacier,** and **Whitney Glacier.**

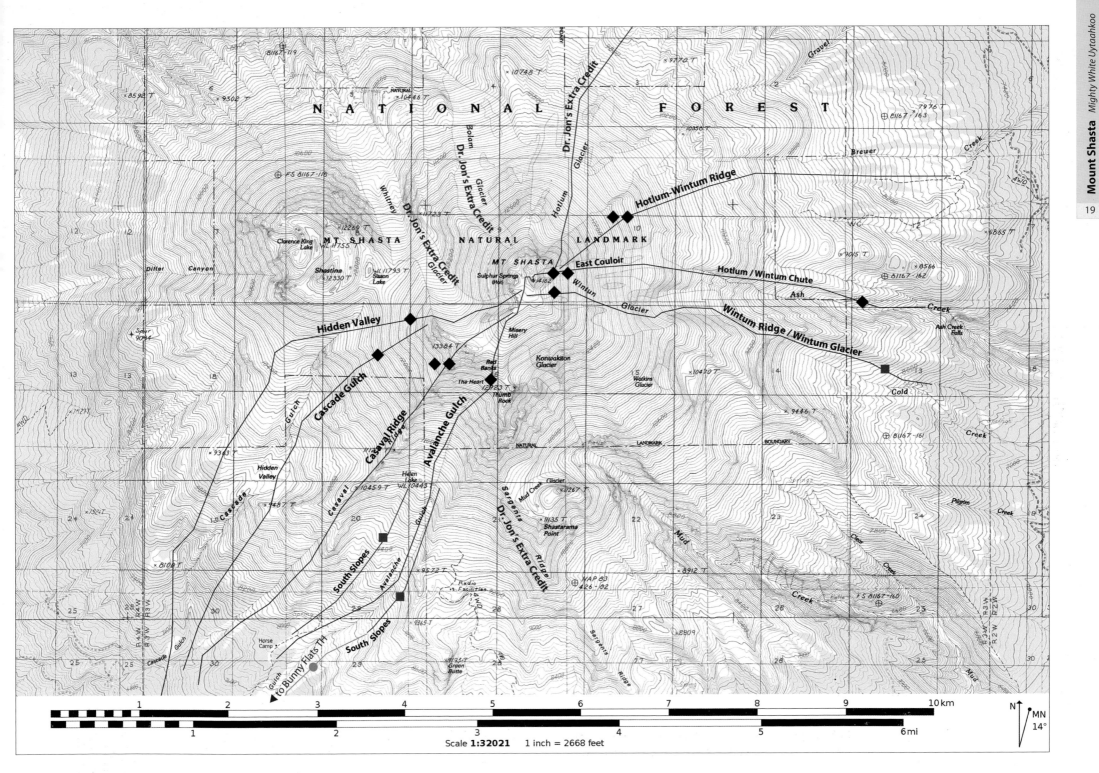

Scale **1:32021**   1 inch = 2668 feet

Lassen Peak

Largest Plug Dome on Earth

10,457 ft | 3,187 m (40° 29' 17" N; 121° 30'18" W)
Bivy and Ski May 2–3, 2014
First Ascent Grover K. Godfrey, 1851
First Ski Descent Unknown

Mount Shasta visible to the north looking across the route climbed on a warm afternoon in California.

Long Climb Via the North Face

After coming off a great summit bivy on Shasta, the Northern California weather forecast showed continued high pressure for at least three more days. I ate tons of food and headed south and east to Lassen Volcanic National Park and decided to take full advantage of the conditions. Lassen Peak was my next goal, named in honor of the Danish blacksmith, Peter Lassen, who guided emigrants past this peak to the Sacramento Valley during the 1830s.

On the morning of May 2nd I decided to give it a go. A relatively late start and a warm spring afternoon allowed me to hike in short sleeves. In the summer, climbing Lassen is pretty routine; its summit can be knocked off relatively easily in only 2,000 vertical feet via its southeast ridge trail from another lake named Helen. In winter and spring the roads in the park are mostly closed off, so you have to enter through the north entrance to the park and climb from the north side of the peak. The road is usually plowed by late March to the Emigrant Pass Trailhead. This approach puts you at a parking lot that is around 6,400 feet elevation, so you have a nice long bushwhack combined with plenty of climbing (4,000 vertical feet) to get to the slopes of Lassen and eventually to the summit.

I figured a short off-trail hike in the woods to the snow line at about 7,000 feet would give me a great shot at some ridiculously sweet lines off the north face of Lassen. With any luck I could ski about 3,500 feet and take home not only a stellar sunset and sunrise, but have an awesome line off that north aspect of the peak. In less than an hour from the parking lot I was through the "devastated area" of former volcanic eruption activity, up to the snow line, and skinning toward the mighty volcano. I had the entire basin and mountain to myself as I headed toward the north ridge proper.

Before I knew it I was savoring the splendid landscape dropping off below me, and I had a nice look at the plentiful ski options off the northeast face while I ascended toward the summit crater of the peak. Mount Shasta appeared in the distance and I breathed a sigh of satisfaction having been up and down that peak a day earlier.

Devastated by Eruptions a Century Ago

Near the summit, the ridge got long and I crossed some rocky outcroppings in an oblong crater that had been formed by several eruptions, the most recent in the early 1900s. In fact, in the month of May, 1914, exactly a hundred years prior, a series of strong explosions began and blew out the area. The rumblings lasted a year, with the most significant of these explosions

Lassen's deep northern summit crater, evidence of the last major eruption in 1915.
Opposite: Main Photo: Sunrise in brutal 50 mph winds.

on May 22, 1915, an eruption that devastated the land that I had ascended that day, stretching all the way back to my vehicle to the north of the volcano.

Nearing the summit of the peak, I nearly fell into a volcano vent crevasse that was covered with snow as I hiked around the crater rim! Steam eased its way up through small cracks in the snow and the rocks, reminding me that this plug dome volcano was currently the most active volcano (with possibly more eruption potential now than St. Helens) in all of the Cascades. Lassen is in fact a dacite plug dome volcano, and about 25,000 years ago it began extruding from the remnants of what was once the Tehama volcano, a stratovolcano that dominated this local landscape and was over 11,000 feet high. (I would be skiing Tehama the next day, so will describe how Tehama formed in the next section.)

Far right: Angular lava towers help divide the northeastern slopes into several broad and spectacular skiable couloirs.
Below: A wavy sunset full of maroon, crimson, and pink indicates strong winds and matches the summit rocks at camp above 10,000 feet.

Impressive Perch as the Southernmost Cascade Volcano

By 2:30 p.m. I had walked to the top in an east to southeast wind that was gusty all afternoon. Once on top I confirmed what I first thought: a line directly off the north face from the very top would be my ski choice come morning. I suspected it should soften up nicely in the sunshine with it being northeast facing. Views of the surrounding landscape featured Mount Shasta to the northwest and Tehama (Brokeoff Mountain) to the south. California's Sacramento Valley farther beyond to the south as well as the northern Sierra Nevada to the south and east were just barely visible on the horizon.

View down the northeast face, lots of ski terrain and room to make turns.

Meteorology of Lassen

Lassen Peak receives some of the heaviest snowfalls in California during the winter and spring, with the snowpack often building up to 25 feet deep near Lake Helen, just south of the peak within Lassen Volcanic National Park. Lassen's southern latitude and modest elevation prevent the development of glaciers, regardless of snowfall. There are only a few small permanent snowfields lasting through the hot summers, making the best time to ski Lassen between March and June, although it can be skied year round. It was very windy that night, likely because of the approach of a cold front within the next 24 to 36 hours. Sometimes wind in the spring on these peaks is strong because there is such a large pressure gradient between centers of high pressure and low pressure in Northern California as the seasons change. The higher the pressure gradients, the stronger the wind.

Among the angular dacite lava blocks, I managed to create a very nice tent platform in the snow, and set my tent up right within the lava blocks on the summit, which provided a little bit of shelter from the wind—becoming stronger and stronger all evening. The sunset light show was brilliant. The redness of the rocks was matched by red clouds in the northern sky. I was treated to a special hour of magic before dark. Once I retired to the tent, the winds pounded me all night and so I barely slept. I was in and out of slumber, and for some reason this peak seemed a lot colder than Shasta despite being almost 4,000 feet lower. At the time it was the lowest bivy of my career to date, but by no means was it easy.

Looking back up the face to gain perspective of where I'd come down from.

Ski Descents and Potential Ski Lines

In the morning I battled the winds and freezing fingers to get some sunrise photos and video, then retired to my tent for a morning nap and some food to allow the conditions to soften a bit. Nevertheless, after a few breakfast snacks, and a less than optimal sunrise (compared to the sunset show), I was ready to ski! Tent and gear all packed up and it was game on for the very steep northeast face. After leaving the summit around 8:30 a.m., I was back to skis off and hiking through the woods to my Tahoe by 10:00 a.m.!

The broad northeast face showing the best ski options Lassen has to offer.

Dr. Jon's Recommendations

◆ **Northeast Face** (9 miles round-trip from Emigrant Pass; 6–8 hours ascent, 1–2 hours descent.) Most years you can take two easy turns directly from the summit cornice between the volcanic lava blocks, and then drop into a shallow but steep gully that gets wider and wider as you descend. The initial 200 feet of skiing can be as steep as 50 degrees. There are a couple of variations once you've dropped onto the face. Skier's left is a larger minor ridge protrusion, and to skier's right you can take on a separate face that is angled slightly to the north. All lines are exceptional, and the angles below the initial 50-degree steepness stay between 35–45 degrees for a couple thousand feet.

■ ● **Northeast Slopes** The Northeast Slopes take you through the devastated area and back to the parking lot at the Emigrant Pass Trailhead in the woods. On a good spring snow year you can make it back to your vehicle in a leisurely hour from the summit.

◆ ■ **North Ridge Below the Northern Summit Crater** This follows the line that I climbed up during my summit bivy (to avoid wet slab snow conditions in the afternoon), which is the north ridge, located west of the northeast face. You can drop northwest off the true summit, ski around the northern edge of the giant crater rim, and follow the north ridge down the peak. North ridge variations include: **a)** Dropping to the east onto the western edge of the northeast face. There are a series of rock buttresses

that divide three or four shallow couloirs down into the basin of the devastated area by way of the northeast face; **b)** You can leave the top of the north ridge early at around 10,000 feet and descend by skiing the **northwest face,** and follow the basins all the way through the forest down Manzanita Creek and Manzanita Lake. Both options provide challenging slope angles of 35–45 degrees but are slightly easier than the northeast face of option 1.

■ ● **Southeast Ridge Trail,** and ◆ ■ **Southeast Face** The standard Lassen Peak Trail rises a mere 2,000 vertical feet and a short 2.5 miles from parking along the road at the well-marked Lassen Peak Trailhead. By late May, from the southern park entrance, the road is plowed all the way to this point near Lake Helen, named for the first woman to climb to the summit of Lassen in 1854. This is the easiest way to access the peak. Both ski routes are descended directly off the summit, the southeast face being slightly steeper and the first skier's left down from the summit rocks, while the southeast ridge trail ski line starts south and east of the flatter summit crater rim plateau. Lake Helen can be an all-day affair, still giving you over 3,500 vertical feet of skiing.

Dr Jon's Extra Credit: These other climbing routes can offer great ski descents, too: **West Face** to the **Manzanita Creek Ski Trail** to the Manzanita Lake Trailhead, **southwest face, south face,** and the nearby **Eagle Peak** (9,222 feet) and **Mount Diller** (9,087 feet).

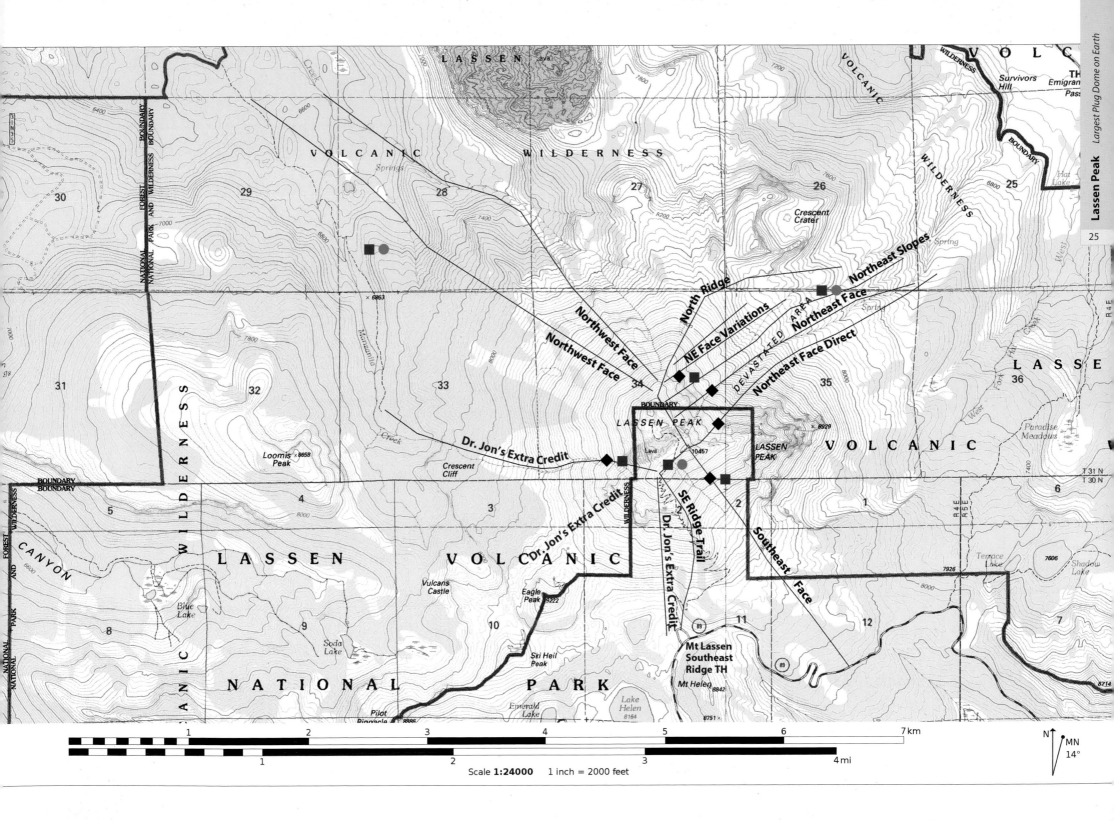

LASSEN · lava

VOLCANIC WILDERNESS

VOLCANIC WILDERNESS

Crescent Crater

Spring

Survivors Hill

Emigrant Pass

Hot Lake

WILDERNESS

BOUNDARY

NATIONAL FOREST AND WILDERNESS

NATIONAL PARK AND WILDERNESS BOUNDARY

Springs

North Ridge

Northeast Slopes

Northwest Face Variations

NE Face Variations

DEVASTATED AREA

Northeast Face

Northwest Face

Northeast Face Direct

Spring

LASSE

BOUNDARY

LASSEN PEAK

LASSEN PEAK

VOLCANIC

Loomis Peak ×8658

Dr. Jon's Extra Credit

Lava 10457

Paradise Meadows

×8929

Crescent Cliff

BOUNDARY BOUNDARY

WILDERNESS

Dr. Jon's Extra Credit

Dr. Jon's Extra Credit

SE Ridge Trail

Southeast Face

LASSEN VOLCANIC

Vulcans Castle

Eagle Peak ×9222

Terrace Lake

Shadow Lake

7926

7606

Blue Lake

CANYON

NATIONAL PARK AND FOREST WILDERNESS

ANIC

Soda Lake

Ski Heil Peak

NATIONAL PARK

Mt Lassen Southeast Ridge TH

Mt Helen ×8842

89

89

8751 ×

Pilot Pinnacle ×8886

Emerald Lake

Lake Helen 8164

8214

Scale **1:24000**   1 inch = 2000 feet

Mount Tehama

Brokeoff Mountain

9,235 ft | 2,815 m (40° 26′ 44″ N; 121° 33′14″ W)
Ski Descent May 3, 2014
First Ascent Unknown
First Ski Descent Unknown

Broad slopes of the South Ridge of Tehama. Lassen Volcano is seen off in the distance.

Second Volcanic Ski Descent in the Same Day

What a morning, and the day was far from over. I continued my tour of Lassen Volcanic National Park and headed for California's third highest volcano. I decided that an afternoon corn ski would do the trick. When I pulled up to the Lassen Chalet Trailhead at 6,700 feet, the mirror temperature gauge on my truck read 57 degrees. I packed a few snacks, my windbreaker, and cameras, and was quickly heading west in the warm afternoon sun in a flash. My thought was that if I could

A thumbs up to signal success from the top of Tehama, second peak of the day to ski.

Left: The lower portion of the South Ridge is easy corn skiing with magnificent views.
Below: Looking back up the South Ridge, the gladed trees leave plenty of room for fun, enjoyable turns.

get this peak done for the afternoon, I would be headed into Oregon in time for the following week's high-pressure weather window that was in the forecast.

On my way up the Forest Lake Ski Trail, tall pine trees blocked the view of my goal. Down to nothing but a short sleeve shirt and I was dripping sweat from the warm sunshine. For the first time I felt like fatigue was setting in—fourth peak in six days, including having skied the fourteener Split Mountain in the Sierras earlier in the week. I was tired, but I also wanted to push myself and see what I was made of for this entire month.

Simple Adversity

Sometimes in life you are going to hit the wall. No matter what, you've got to find ways to put a smile on your face and just give it your best effort. That day was tough. Having just come off of Lassen and a night with no sleep due to high winds, I was at the end of my physical limit. As I ascended the peak that day, I would simply pick trees in the distance or perhaps a rock or a ridgeline, and just make that my basic goal for the time being. Next thing I knew I was taking off my skis and packing them on my back for the final 500 vertical feet up the south face of Brokeoff Mountain. Views and getting closer to a summit usually makes me stronger—I get excited! Time seemed to go by so fast that afternoon. Around 4:00 p.m. I was on the top of my third California peak, and pushing through the temporary suffering was very much worth the views!

Lassen Volcanic Complex

Mount Tehama was originally formed as part of the Lassen Volcanic Complex, an area of active volcanism for at least three million years. Today's Brokeoff Mountain (9,235 feet) is much lower than what the giant Mount Tehama stratovolcano (11,000 feet) once was. Looking north toward Mount Lassen, I could see the large area that once contained this ancient volcano: today it includes the current peaks of Mount Diller and Eagle Peak. Following Mount Tehama's collapse thousands of years ago, glaciers from the last ice age also carved out steep sides and deep valleys in the nearby areas. If you venture to the areas contained in Lassen Volcanic National Park, it is possible to find active hydrothermal features such as Sulphur Works and Bumpass Hell, which are evidence that magma still underlies this area.

Ski Descents and Potential Ski Lines

While a bivy of this peak wasn't necessary (it's merely a volcanic remnant of Lassen itself), it did provide me with about 2,500 feet more vertical skiing in the same day as I had skied Lassen, as well as awesome views of Lassen and Shasta to boot. While Mount Tehama can be considered an undervalued and low-profile ski objective, it is a great peak that offers spectacular views and moderately difficult terrain. Due to easy year-round access from the Lassen Park road and south entrance, the mountain is a great winter climb and ski.

Dr. Jon's Recommendations

◆■ **South Ridge** The gentle summit slopes give way to pine trees that are far enough apart to give you plenty of room to navigate the steepest sections of the ridge. The face along the ridgeline gives you several options. After about 500 feet of 35–40-degree skiing, you can ski glades of meadows and treed sections veering toward Forest Lake to the east (skier's left) and then find your way back to the trailhead by taking the Forest Lake Ski Trail back to your vehicle. This tour is about 12 miles round-trip and 2,500 vertical feet.

■● **West Ridge Trail,** and ■ **Southwest Face** The standard Tehama Peak Trail is covered by snow, but you can take a westerly line down the gentle slopes of the mountain and have about 500 vertical feet of great corn skiing in mid-day or afternoon sunlight. If you prefer, climb up onto the far western prominent summit of this ridgeline and take in the views. Next, drop off the southwest face. Once reaching thicker trees at the base of the southwest face, be sure to traverse skier's left (east), and join the south ridge route described above and ski out to your vehicle by way of the Forest Lake Ski Trail.

◆◆ **Southeast Face Variation** Follow the south ridge route for the first 300 to 400 feet below the summit, then take a sharp skier's left to pick your way out onto or below the cliffs that guard Tehama's southeast face. Some years the snow coverage is good enough to allow steep passage through these cliff bands. You may have to get creative. You can also just bypass the cliffs via the south ridge and then traverse to the steep but skiable slopes below them. This route joins the south ridge route at the base of the face.

Dr Jon's Extra Credit: Check out the nearby **Eagle Peak** (9,222 feet) and **Mount Diller** (9,087 feet). If you want to get really extreme, take a look at the various cliffs and couloirs that guard **Brokeoff Mountain's** north face and north aspects of the west ridge, too. In particular, check out the steep, narrow north-facing —up to almost 70 degrees at the top, and technical.

Taking a short break to scout the Brokeoff Couloir. Mount Shasta is in the clouds in the distance.

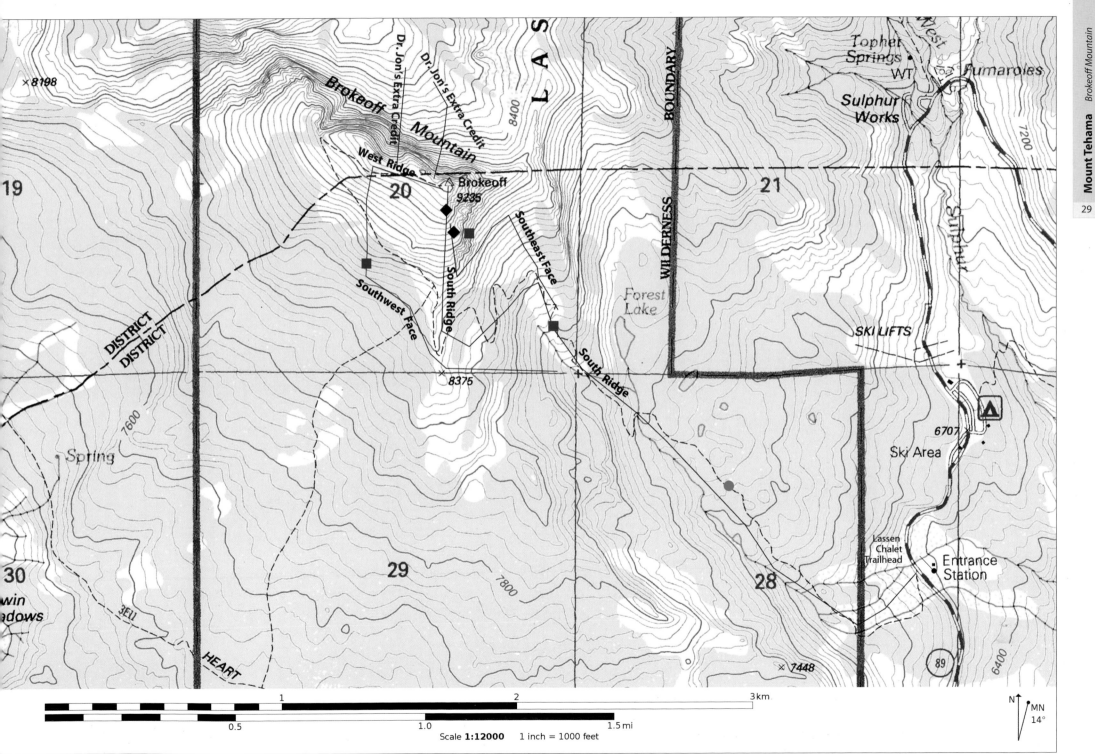

Scale **1:12000**   1 inch = 1000 feet

Curtin

Willamette
National
Forest

58

La Pine

Deschutes
National
Forest

20

5

97

Diamond Peak

138

Roseburg

Umpqua
National
Forest

Mount
Thielsen

Chemult

Diamond
Lake

Winema
National
Forest

Silver Lake

138

Crater Lake
National Park

Crater Lake

Mount Scott

Mount Garfield

Applegate Peak

5

Rogue River
National
Forest

97

395

Lake
Abert

Grants Pass

Mount
McLoughlin

Upper
Kalamath
Lake

199

140

Valley Falls

Medford

Beatty

140

Ashland

Klamath
Falls

5

OREGON

CALIFORNIA

Klamath
National
Forest

Lakeview

97

395

N

Goose
Lake

0   12.5   25 Miles

96

39

Clear Lake
Reservoir

"Dr. Kedrowski has become a master at setting up exposed camps, chiseling tent platforms and using ice blocks to melt his tent into the snow. This was especially true on Mt. Thielsen, a magical looking spire with no room for a tent. It's all great training for the world's highest peaks, plus an opportunity to study the unique geology of volcanic craters and ever-shifting weather. It leads to amazing photographs, too!"
—**JASON BLEVINS,** *The Denver Post*

Top right: Crater Lake
Bottom right: Diamond Peak

Mount McLoughlin

The Old Chief Storm Factor

9,495 ft | 2,894 m (42° 26′ 40″ N; 122° 18′ 56″ W)
Ski Descent May 5, 2014
First Ascent Unknown, likely Native Americans
First Ski Descent Unknown

Zach Taylor looks down the north bowl from the summit with Klamath Lake in the distance. Photo by Ayn-Marie Halicka
Right: the tallest conifer trees at this elevation indicate the prevailing westerly winds.

A New Unknown Volcano and a New State

I had to wait patiently for a few days as a storm moved through southern Oregon bringing rain and snow to the region. On the morning of May 4, I parked my vehicle at the top of a pass near Four Mile Lake Road in the middle of nowhere off of State Highway 140 in Oregon. It was raining and the weather was socked in, so rather than trying to find my way through the woods and eventually to the top of Mount McLoughlin for the night, I spent the day in the back of my Tahoe, reading, writing, napping, and eating. When the time passed that I knew I needed to make it to the summit before dark, I decided to spend the night at the trailhead and get a fresh start by the morning of the 5th.

Deep sleep normally occurs when you are isolated and in a parking lot that is devoid of other cars. The rain paddles the roof of your vehicle,

The author on the summit in a whiteout.

and passes you off to a pleasant slumber. When I finally woke on May 5 it was Cinco de Mayo, but deep in the Pacific Northwest, there was nothing to celebrate. I had to start a long 6-mile and 5,000-foot vertical climb to the top of McLoughlin by hiking through the woods in Solomon sneakers on the Pacific Crest Trail. I was convinced that I had a higher chance of seeing Bigfoot that day than another person. I carried overnight gear plus my skis and boots on my pack, as I would have to switch over to skins and skis once I reached the snow line on the McLoughlin Peak Trail. Carrying everything made for a heavy pack.

Springtime Weather in Southern Oregon Oregon weather can be fickle. The seasonal change brings on strong, intense storms that can sometimes stall out over the southern Oregon peaks because of their high elevation compared to coastal lowland valleys to the west and the central Oregon desert to the east. These storms often create zero visibility, strong winds, and short intense snowfall events. Even though it was forecasted to be clearing, the lingering effects of the storm that had lasted for three days were hanging on to McLoughlin as I ascended the steady east ridge.

Above 7,000 feet the weather was socked in. As the trees became thinner and thinner, the visibility dropped to less than 50 feet. The snow began to fall, and I was suddenly in an all-out blizzard. Keeping slightly south of the east ridge as I climbed, I approached the last dwarfs of the treeline. Here the angle of the ridge increased to about 35 degrees, and skinning was difficult. I ducked behind the last tree I could find and assessed the situation. I would at least get up to the summit in the blizzard, and I could always retreat quickly on skis, so I pushed on.

Making the Summit Despite All Odds

With skis on my pack, I put my head down and steadily climbed as hard as I could. I could've been on another continent for all I knew, because I could barely see the snow on the slopes above as I climbed. I had all my overnight gear so if worse came to worst I felt like I could just dig in on the summit and find a way to make the best of it, gaining shelter by quickly putting my tent up or just building a snow cave.

Making the summit despite the blizzard, I glanced at the time: 4:00 p.m. I took off my pack, switched the bindings into ski mode, and looked around a bit. My altimeter read too high at 9,700 feet and when I took a 50-yard stroll in pounding winds on a giant broad cornice, the western side of the summit top dropped off into nothing. "This has to be it," I shouted, "but no way am I staying here!"

As much as I wanted to stay, I knew the right choice was to click in and follow my tracks back down the east ridge before they became covered in fresh snow, which could seal my fate. As hard as the decision was, I knew I had to go. With my hands freezing as I shot some quick summit video, I quickly turned off the camera, rolled my camera goggles to record, and started down off the snowy butte and into the white room. It was a bittersweet

Visibility was very poor above the timber.

The entire face of the Northeast Bowls offer several excellent ski lines. Photo by Ayn-Marie Halicka. Below: The author's turns along the top of the southeast face after leaving the summit in a blizzard.

summit, but I knew I had a lot more peaks to do, so staying the night up on McLoughlin wasn't worth the risk. As elusive as this summit was for John McLoughlin to fathom climbing when he saw it from the neighboring trading posts in the lower Klamath valley as Chief Factor for the Hudson's Bay Company in the 1830s, I was fortunate to make it to the top and reap the benefits of a rewarding ski descent to safety.

Ski Descents and Potential Ski Lines

While a bivy of this peak didn't happen (Mother Nature decides), it did provide me with about 3,000 more vertical feet of skiing nearly back to the Pacific Crest Trail. Once I dropped down below 8,000 feet on the east slopes, the storm abated, and the nicely spaced trees made for an excellent and fast ride down to the safety of the forest. Due to easy access from Oregon 140 and the PCT, as well as a high trailhead elevation (5,500 feet), Mount McLoughlin provides a great climb in all seasons and a full-length ski descent back to your vehicle in the winter months.

Dr. Jon's Recommendations

◆ ■ **East Ridge** The ski descent follows the ridge and skirts the steep rocky portions of the ridge on the skier's right (south) side. Steeper slopes ease to 20–30 degrees and give way to pine trees in nice glades. The lower reaches of the mountain along the Mount McLoughlin Trail and the Pacific Crest Trail are gentle and easy going to get you back to your vehicle at the Fourmile Lakes Trailhead or farther south near Oregon Highway 140 and the PCT at the start of Forest Road 3650 (11 miles round-trip and 4,000 vertical skiing can be done in 6–8 hours).

◆◆/◆ **Northeast Bowls** These classic bowls give McLoughlin a lofty status as one of the best volcanoes to ski in all of the Pacific Northwest. From the summit, a direct line to the east and off the initial summit ridge will get you to the top of the northeast aspect of the peak. Then the choice is yours: you can ski the largest and longest of the broad but steep 45-degree couloirs by staying to skier's right, but the entire bowl has numerous lines that will drop you into the trees. Once to the base of the bowls, take a right turn and ski east to rejoin the Mount McLoughlin Trail and the PCT to get back to the trailhead at Oregon Highway 140 (4,000 vertical skiing and 12–13 miles for a 7–12 hour day). You can also ski or hike out to the east to the Fourmile Lake Trailhead, which shortens this route significantly in May or June.

◆ ■ **Southeast Face** This line is up to 40 degrees and steep for the first couple hundred feet off the summit but then stays 35 degrees or less and then follows an opening (former avalanche path) into the trees. Crafty tree skiing in a southeast direction will bring you back to your vehicle at the PCT Trailhead at Oregon 140. This line gets lots of sun in the spring, so descend before 10:00 a.m. if you can.

◆ ■ **Southwest Face** Slightly steeper and a bit more narrow and difficult than the southeast face route, this impressive line is direct and gives you a complete 4,200-foot descent for an excellent sunny spring corn run in March or April and will bring you all the way back to your vehicle at the Lava Flow Rye Spring Trailhead at 5,200 feet, which begins where Forest Road 3740 ends. You may be able to ski down the forest road depending on how early in the spring you go.

◆ ■ **North Bowl** Directly off the summit, a short traverse of the abrupt north ridge gives you access to the spectacular north bowl where a couple of different lines await your exploration. Once you reach the trees, veer to skier's left (northwest) and ski to your vehicle at the Twin Ponds Trailhead (Forest Road 3760).

Dr Jon's Extra Credit: The **northwest ridge** and face is a long and wild alternative to the standard approaches and is rarely ever skied. Use the Twin Ponds Trailhead by driving up Forest Road 3760.

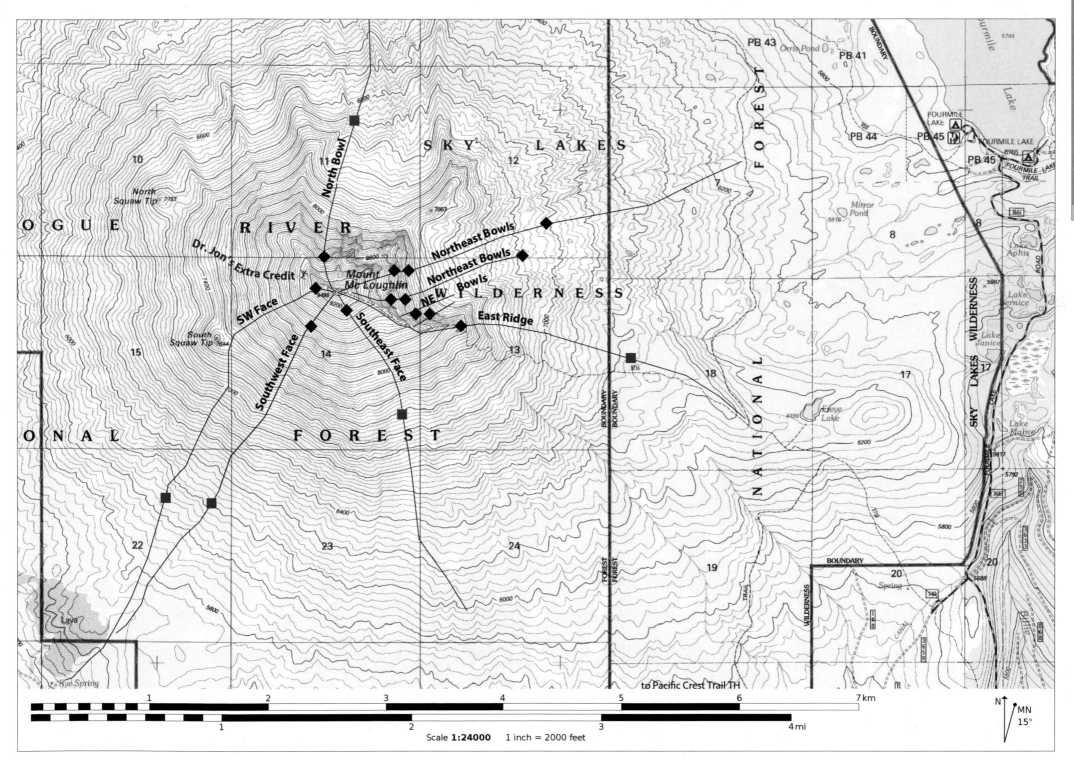

PB 43

Orris Pond   PB 41

S K Y   L A K E S

12

FOURMILE LAKE

PB 44   PB 45

PB 45

FOURMILE LAKE

Mirror Pond

10

North Squaw Tip

11   North Bowl

O G U E   R I V E R

8

8

Lake Aphis

Dr. Jon's Extra Credit

Northeast Bowls

Northeast Bowls

Mount McLoughlin

NEW Bowls

W I L D E R N E S S

Lake Bernice

SW Face

South Squaw Tip

Southwest Face

Southeast Face

East Ridge

15

14

13

18

17

Lake Janice

Fuleye Lake

Lake Malice

N A T I O N A L

BOUNDARY   BOUNDARY

O N A L

F O R E S T

22   23   24   19   20

FOREST   FOREST

TRAIL

BOUNDARY

WILDERNESS

Spring

20

SKY LAKES WILDERNESS

CANAL

Lava

to Pacific Crest Trail TH

Rye Spring

| 1 | 2 | 3 | 4 | 5 | 6 | 7 km |

| 1 | 2 | 3 | 4 mi |

Scale **1:24000**   1 inch = 2000 feet

N   MN 15°

Crater Lake National Park

Mount Mazama **6,173 ft** | **1,881 m** (42° 55' 76" N; 122° 00' 19" W)

A Vanished Volcano

Below: Crater Lake at dawn, Mount Scott on the Horizon to the right.
Opposite: The Park covered in a thick mantle of snow as Wizard Island is seen from the Crater Rim.

Nearly 8,000 years ago, an enormous volcano reigned supreme as the highest in Oregon (over 12,000 feet); it was the largest in volume in all of the Pacific Northwest. Imagine the ski potential of that giant mountain! Even though it took about 500,000 years for the stratovolcano to form, the destruction of the towering peak only took a few days. Blasts of rock, pumice, ash, and hot gasses protruded from vents along the volcano's periphery and allowed massive amounts of magma to drain from the chambers deep inside the peak. Without any support from within the volcano, the mountain collapsed. The basin that was created filled with water and is the present day Crater Lake.

Wizard Island, a volcanic cinder cone, formed after a smaller eruption a few thousand years later. The lake itself is 6 miles across and 2,000 feet deep, the deepest lake in the United States. While the weather isn't always ideal for skiing to some of the highest features in Crater Lake National Park, including Mount Scott (8,926 feet), Dutton Ridge (8,147 feet), Applegate Peak (8,126 feet), and Mount Garfield (8,048 feet), all of these small peaks are worthy ski objectives. If you wanted to try and ski Wizard Island, you would need an inflatable raft, which would be an adventure! The Park Service prohibits ski descents into the crater rim, and you can see why—the avalanche danger is pretty extreme within the caldera.

Mount Scott
Highest Point in Crater Lake National Park

8,938 ft | 2,724 m (42° 55′ 22″ N; 122° 00′ 59″ W)
Ski Descent May 6, 2014
Bivy September 5–6, 2015 (on the back side of Mount Scott, in a legal camping zone)
First Ascent Unknown, likely Native Americans
First Ski Descent Unknown

Long Failure of a Slog on Skis

I drove through rain and snow arriving late to Crater Lake National Park on the night of May 5th. I was hoping that the storm would stop on that day, but the snow at high elevations never quit. Waking up to a blizzard on the morning of the 6th, I decided to at least attempt Mount Scott, the highest point in the park and one of the most scenic viewpoints for any national park. There is a fire lookout on top of the peak that I definitely wanted to take a look at as well. Mount Scott was named for an 1800s pioneer named Levi Scott, who was responsible for founding the town of Scottsburg, Oregon.

After a hot breakfast of oatmeal and a comforting cup of hot chocolate, the snow appeared to be letting up, so I decided to begin the long 29-mile round-trip journey to Mount Scott at 3:00 a.m. The landscape surrounding Crater Lake within Crater Lake National Park is uniquely vast and beautiful. But in the early hours of May 6, I wasn't being treated to any sort of views with the snow falling heavily and the darkness consuming my life. There are a series of small peaks that make up the caldera rim around Crater Lake. While bypassing Garfield Peak, Applegate Peak, and Dutton Ridge, the pre-dawn light gave me glimpses of the steep avalanche paths along the buried Park Service road called Rim Drive. While I wasn't too worried here about avalanches in May, I could see how these peaks could catch an unsuspecting snowshoer or ski mountaineer off guard while out on an enjoyable winter retreat in the park.

First rays over the lake on a cold May morning.

Around first light it began to snow heavily. The lake was obscured from some of the common viewpoints along Rim Drive as I skinned toward Mount Scott. By 9:00 a.m. I had made it around the southern end of the lake to the eastern rim near a point called Cloud Cap. It was still dumping snow and there were no tracks to be found—I was all alone. I knew Mount Scott's summer trailhead wasn't far from where I stood but I couldn't see anything. Snowdrifts were nearly up to my waist as I tried to skin eastward toward my goal. As I struggled it also dawned on me that the past couple of days had been very tough on me. I had some success on Mount McLoughlin but I was completely blasted on that peak and was lucky to get back down on skis in that blizzard. If I went any farther today, I didn't know if I had the power to make it back before nightfall. About 12 miles had passed and I threw in the towel. I felt defeated. Could I find my way back to the park headquarters where I parked my Tahoe? It was suddenly my only option. At only 8,000 feet, somewhere near the base of the northwest bowl on Mount Scott, I had surrendered. It was a noble attempt, but it also motivated me to return someday and ski off its summit on a sunny day when I could really enjoy the views of Crater Lake.

USGS benchmark on Mount Scott's summit.

That day was a great lesson for me. It can also serve as a lesson for all of us. *Failure is only failure if you let it become failure.* I believed better weather would come and I also knew that I had to move on to the next mountain. Life can be like that sometimes, if an experience is hindering you for too long, you should be ready to seek out a better opportunity and not be afraid to move past your struggles to chase your next goal. I had many more peaks to climb and ski on this long trip, so I pushed with all my strength back around Crater Lake and found myself safely back to my vehicle by late afternoon. I was exhausted but knew that the next day would be a new day with new opportunity.

A brilliant shade of color after sunset at the fire lookout.

Crater Lake and
Wizard Island

Sunrise across central Oregon.
Below: Many tent sites in the
National Park have nice views,
backcountry camping permit
required.

A Rewarding Sunrise

I went to bed that night exhausted and slept soundly. While camping near the lake that night, before heading to another peak the next day, the storm abated and the stars came out. The next morning I woke to an impressive sunrise over the caldera and felt new strength to continue on. I didn't have time to waste, so I headed farther north, out of Crater Lake National Park and toward my next objective, Mount Thielsen.

Mount Scott Summit Sunset

In late summer 2015, I ventured back to Crater Lake and Mount Scott to camp in the backcountry of the park. I was rewarded with a brilliant sunset and a stunning pink sunrise when I climbed to the top of Scott in light winds for the magical hour at dusk and dawn from the infamous fire lookout.

Ski Descents and Potential Ski Lines

Crater Lake National Park is a destination for great ski tours. While it's tough to find a ski line on any of the peaks along the crater rim of the lake to exceed 1,000 feet, Crater Lake National Park offers nearly unlimited ski touring potential. One of the best ski tours is a circumnavigation of the lake. Each year about a hundred brave souls attempt to travel all the way around the lake on either skis or snowshoes. Although the circuit can be accomplished all winter long, most parties wait until March, April, or May due to longer days and better weather. Crater Lake gets an average of 40 feet of snow per winter, so the weather is not good for extended periods in the winter! Mount Scott is the highest and most vertical peak for a ski descent, but shorter climb-and-ski options include Garfield, Applegate, and Dutton, as well as a few others (I was able to ski Garfield in a whiteout in 2014). One thing is certain: your rewarding views of the lake will be ever-changing—sunrise and sunset are particularly stunning, but you could set eyes on Crater Lake each hour of each day and have a completely different view every time.

Sunrise or sunset can offer the best views of the entire Park. Mount Scott's northeast bowl is visible.

Dr. Jon's Recommendations

◆■ **Mount Scott** This is a long ski descent in the winter months because you have to travel nearly 14 miles just to reach the base of the mountain from park headquarters, as Rim Drive is closed. Once you've cracked the code and made the approach to the base of the mountain, your safest ascent option of Mount Scott is along the Mount Scott Trail, which wraps around the southwest side of the peak. Ski descent options include the broad **northwest bowl,** the **north face, east face,** and the **southeast face.** Bear in mind that you'll have to retrace your slog around Crater Lake at the end of the day, so choose your descent wisely as to not add even more distance to your trek. I would say the most straightforward ski option is indeed the northwest bowl back toward the Mount Scott Trailhead. This peak is probably best climbed and skied in the winter with an overnight snow camp somewhere between Cloud Cap (8,065 feet) and the summer Mount Scott Trailhead to the northwest of the peak. Skiing Mount Scott in late May or early June, when the road is open, is likely the easiest way to ski the peak without all the extra miles.

■● **Garfield Peak / Applegate Peak** These classic summits right up close to the crater rim give you a bird's eye view of the lake and are both only 6.5 miles round-trip, making for a quick and fun adventure on skis.

From park headquarters at 6,450 feet, travel southeast and then east on Rim Drive for almost 2 miles. You will then head due north leaving Rim Drive at a high point on the road before the road drops in elevation. The final 1.4 miles to either Applegate Peak to the northeast or Garfield Peak to the northwest are both an elevation gain of about 1,000 feet from the road through open meadows and groves of trees and gradually steeper terrain.

◆■ **Circumnavigation** This is rated into the Black Diamond category because it is a long 31-mile trip to ski around Crater Lake. When the weather is clear, the loop that starts and ends at the Rim Village (7,100 feet) takes an average of three days (two overnight camps) to complete. Storms can force many parties to turn back or force an extra night. The route can be unmarked, difficult to follow in places, and you will be required to pass through many avalanche paths. You should be experienced in winter camping, backcountry travel, and avalanche safety, and don't forget to obtain your backcountry permit from the park headquarters where you can also start your adventure if you don't park at Rim Village.

Dr Jon's Extra Credit: Heading west and northwest to the west end of Crater Lake you can climb to **Wizard Island Overlook, Watchman Peak** (8,013 feet), or **Hillman Peak** (8,151 feet). From here you can catch a magnificent sunrise over Wizard Island and Crater Lake.

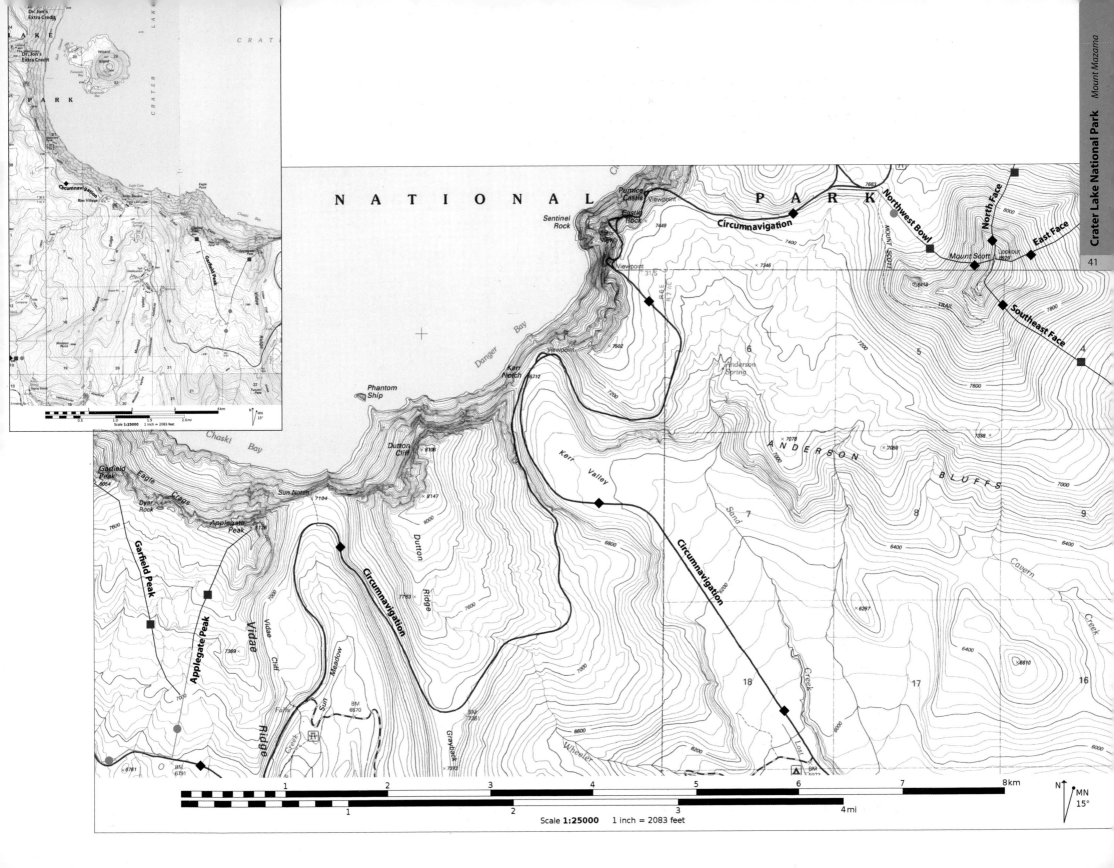

NATIONAL PARK

Circumnavigation

Northwest Bowl

North Face

East Face

Southeast Face

Mount Scott

Pumice Castle

Viewpoint

Sentinel Rock

Castle Rock

Viewpoint

Danger Bay

Kerr Notch

Phantom Ship

Kerr Valley

ANDERSON

Anderson Spring

BLUFFS

Chaski Bay

Dutton Cliff

Sun Notch

Dutton Ridge

Circumnavigation

Circumnavigation

Garfield Peak

Eagle Crags

Dyar Rock

Applegate Peak

Garfield Peak

Applegate Peak

Vidae Cliff

Sun Meadow

Vidae Falls

Sun Creek

Graybeck

Wheeler

Cavern Creek

Lost Creek

Sand Creek

Scale **1:25000**   1 inch = 2083 feet

N MN 15°

Mount Thielsen

Lightning Rod of the Cascades

9,182 ft | 2,799 m (43° 09′ 10″ N; 122° 03′59″W)
Bivy and Ski May 7–8, 2014
First Ascent E.E. Hayden, 1883
First Ski Descent Unknown

Summit camp just below the spire.

A Spire Known as Big Cowhorn

After a gorgeous morning at Crater Lake, I headed north up the road for about an hour and came to one of the most intimidating looking peaks in the Cascades. Mount Thielsen may be less than 10,000 feet high, but it looks foreboding and dangerous. It also looks like something out of Lord of the Rings or Harry Potter fantasy-world fiction story—a towering and pointy volcanic spire with steep drops on nearly all sides.

Weather forecasts showed that the bluebird weather of Wednesday morning wasn't going to last for more than twenty-four hours. In fact, after studying some forecasts, and getting a confirmation from Meteorologist Chris Tomer, I had a feeling that storms would come in the following morning, so climbing the peak was going to become a significant risk. Well, I have had my fair share of summit bivys over the years and I knew that as long as the weather was good to get to the top and get a camp established, then I would be able to come down in bad weather. I also was confident that there wouldn't be lightning in this snowstorm system. Even in some of the worst conditions in Colorado, Pakistan, or in Nepal on Everest, I have an uncanny sense of direction, perception of the terrain, and unique memorization for route finding. I literally memorize every feature on the mountain as I ascend, and I carefully script out an escape plan for when I arrive on a summit. I had just been through this a couple days earlier on McLoughlin, so I wasn't worried I could execute my plan on Thielsen.

Approaching Thielsen from the southwest along Oregon Hwy 230.

Diamond Lake and Mount Bailey come into view upon exiting the trees.

Climbing and Executing a Plan on an Extinct Volcano

For Thielsen I would carefully follow my own rules and make sure I got to the top safely in good weather. I ate a good breakfast and started up through the woods on the Thielsen Trail at 10:00 a.m. in the warm and clear Oregon sunshine. The peaks of Diamond, Howlock, Bachelor, and the Three Sisters became visible to the north as I ascended the west ridge, which was getting steeper and steeper. There was no wind and I was kind of in my own world. A fading skin track from a duo of skiers from the day before gave me a nice little track to follow, but at times I would deviate and make my own path.

At 8,600 feet, I took a break on a rock on the steep south face of the peak and enjoyed the views to the south: Bailey, Crater Lake, Mount Scott, and McLoughlin all were visible. It felt good to be up near the top, and I was beginning to familiarize myself with the Oregon landscape. A quick switch to crampons, and I loaded my skis on my pack. Overnight gear and skis made me feel slow, but this being my seventh peak to ski off of since the start of May, I was feeling pretty strong. Still being at relatively low elevation, I was moving efficiently. I climbed a pair of gullies back-to-back and reached the summit ridge, then took an ascending traverse to the west into the top gully to reach the summit spire and eventually up the Class 5, 80-foot summit ridge.

Most Incredible Bivy Site Yet

I spied a potential bivy site. It was out of the way of any of the snow and ice melting off the fulgurite* spire and it was not in the summit gully. I set my pack down and looked at the options. There was no room for a tent on the top of the extinct volcanic summit spire block 80 feet above me. Still, I took a water bottle and grabbed my ice axe and took a few minutes to solve the puzzle up the Class 5 rock pitch. It was a little tricky on the wind-blown, snow-crystallized ice that coated the rock, but the warm sunny day had melted off much of the ice and it was mostly just bare rock.

In a flash I pulled myself up to the top of the spire. Wow! What a brilliant view in all directions and a crystal clear afternoon with only light colorful clouds to the north. Glaciers had spent thousands of years carving out this sharp spire that I stood upon, giving Thielsen its pinnacle shape. It honestly made my stomach drop as there was quite a bit of air off the summit to the north and east. I didn't linger for long. After all, I had to get my camp set up. So I took a drink from my bottle and down-climbed back to where I would put my tent.

Safely off the summit spire, I set to work. Because the angle of the snow and ice was 30 degrees or so, I chopped out a platform and redistributed the snow to make a nice 4-foot by 8-foot site to put the tent on. This took a couple hours, so from about 2:00 to 4:00 p.m. I worked to make sure the platform was large enough to fit my tent. On a few occasions I would pause to eat a snack and take in the views. I actually couldn't help but pretend that this was like putting in some wild and dangerous camp on one of the peaks in the Himalaya or Karakoram. In fact, sometimes it felt like I was back in Pakistan on my expedition to the Gasherbrums from the previous year. What incredible training this would be for the future!—although, when chopping the platform, it was much easier to breathe at 9,100 feet than at over 20,000 feet.

Soon I had the platform ready and was starting to fish for rocks on the ledge to help secure the tent. I used my ice axe and my ski poles on three of the tent arms. Part of the rock spire ridge would shield me from the wind and also keep me from rolling off the vertical west side of the peak. In the morning all I would have to do is down-climb 15 feet into a flat portion of the couloir on a snowbank and carefully cut some turns to make my escape. It was a perfect campsite! By 5:00 p.m. I was cozy in my tent and warm in the afternoon sun. I took some time to melt snow and ice for drinks and made some soup for dinner. Eating always comes easily on projects like this and I had worked up quite an appetite. By 7:00 p.m. the sky began to darken. It had an eerie feel as I knew there was a rain and snowstorm approaching from the Pacific on the horizon. In about thirty minutes the summit and surrounding Cascades would become engulfed in fog, so I snapped a few photos and retired for the night.

*Fulgurite is a substance that forms when lightning strikes and melts rock. In the mid-1800s, a Polish settler and early explorer of the area named Jon Hurlburt observed lightning strikes over the peak and was fascinated by the phenomenon. He later chatted about what happened with his good friend, engineer Hans Thielsen. Somehow the stories of lightning were spread after that by Thielsen and Hurlburt and the name of the mountain stuck.

A foggy afternoon obscures the view.

The author chopped out and built a nice, relatively level tent platform just below the summit with views of Diamond Lake below.

The Great Escape from the Top

I actually slept very well, and woke around 3:00 a.m. to the sound of wind, snow, and freezing rain on the tent. "Uh oh," I thought, "I certainly hope the weather isn't so bad that I can't get off this peak safely."

At 4:45 a.m., at first light, I snuck outside to take a look in the 40 mph winds. I was on guard about the fact that I was fogged in and getting drilled by the storm. Back inside at 5:00 a.m. I started packing. I knew this weather was going to last for the next five days, so getting down sooner rather than later was the solution. I stuffed my sleeping bag and put on my ski boots. I got everything packed while eating a pack of Nutter Butter cookies, drinking some Powerade, and downing a PB&J. All set to get down!

I tossed my pack out and set it on the ledge at 6:00 a.m. I couldn't see much in the waxing light. It was foggy, but I was able to snap a few photos before ripping down the tent. I used my ice axe to loosen the frozen rocks that were holding the tent into place. Fortunately I left plenty of room in the top of my pack to stuff the tent. (I would worry about drying it and folding it properly later.) All the while the wind threatened to toss me off the ledge! Minutes later I crab-walked down to the safe landing area at the top of the couloir (I had even memorized the handholds on the rock the night before) and clicked into my skis. I would be down pretty quickly now! A few icy turns, but the snow was actually not too bad. I had memorized every part of the route down and in a few minutes was down to the trees and onto the actual west ridge. I knew where to go now. Soon it was snowing lightly, and in less than 30 minutes after leaving my summit camp, I was into the forest. It felt good to get back into the woods, smell the pine, and make my way back to my vehicle at the trailhead amid rainy drizzle to a second breakfast.

Snow and freezing drizzle blur the camera lens during descent.

Ski Descents and Potential Ski Lines

It really isn't possible to ski directly from the summit of Thielsen, but there are a handful of lines off of the peak. The best terrain utilizes a number of glacially cut faces and gully systems that start from the base of the volcanic spire. The best access to Mount Thielsen is by using the Mount Thielsen Trailhead and Trail 1456, located just 3 miles southwest of the village of Diamond Lake on Oregon Highway 138. In fact, the trailhead is right near the southeast corner of Diamond Lake itself.

Northwest Facing Bowl provides excellent skiing. Far right: Just below the simmit spire, the south face begins as one narrow colouir, later opening to two separate gullies.

A great view of Thielsen and the Northwest Facing Bowl (left) while skinning up the West Ridge.

Dr. Jon's Recommendations

◆ ■ **South Face** Once you down-climb the summit spire, the obvious narrow gully opens on skier's left to a broader face with a choice of a pair of wider gullies that never exceed 40 degrees. One of the best lines drops directly from a small col to the southeast of some significant pinnacles that are also part of the summit massif. Once down to the thicker trees you will have to traverse to skier's right (west) in order to meet the Thielsen Trail and get back to the trailhead.

◆ ■ **Northwest Facing Bowl** From about 500 to 700 feet below the summit (from your descent of the southwest face), get onto the west ridge. Off of the west ridge to the skier's right you'll peer off the ridge and down into the steep northwest-facing bowl. From the west ridge, look for a series of notches that allow for cliff-free access into the northwest bowl. Choose a line that best suits your ability and ski some stellar terrain back down to the trees. Stay parallel to the west ridge to ski directly west and find the Mount Thielsen Trail to get back to the trailhead.

◆ ■ **Southwest Face / West Ridge** You can start at about 9,100 feet at the base of the summit pinnacle. There is a nice wind-blown snow feature most years, and the start of a couloir that narrows and widens to the entire southwest face of Thielsen. Skier's left is the south face, and then about 300 feet below the true summit, take a gully to skier's right and this will lead you toward the west ridge and some krummholz trees. Follow your skin track back into the woods along the ridge and enjoy the gladed terrain through the forest along the Thielsen Trail and back to your vehicle (this route is about 10 miles round-trip and 3,700' vertical skiing).

◆ ■ **North Facing Bowls / Lathrop Glacier** This is rated into the Black Diamond category because it is a long approach via the Howlock Trail to Thielsen Meadows, Thielsen Camp, and the PCT. Steep snow climbing in the north-facing basin on the Lathrop glacier will get you to about 1,000 feet below the summit spire where you can put on your skis and drop a couple thousand feet of skiing.

Dr Jon's Extra Credit: From a saddle on the south ridge of Thielsen at about 8,800 ft, you might just be able to choose a line that takes you into the **east** basin of Thielsen. But, once you drop over to that other side of the mountain, you are a long way from where you parked. Good luck and be safe exploring the faraway basin of **Cottonwood Creek** south of **Hollys Ridge!**

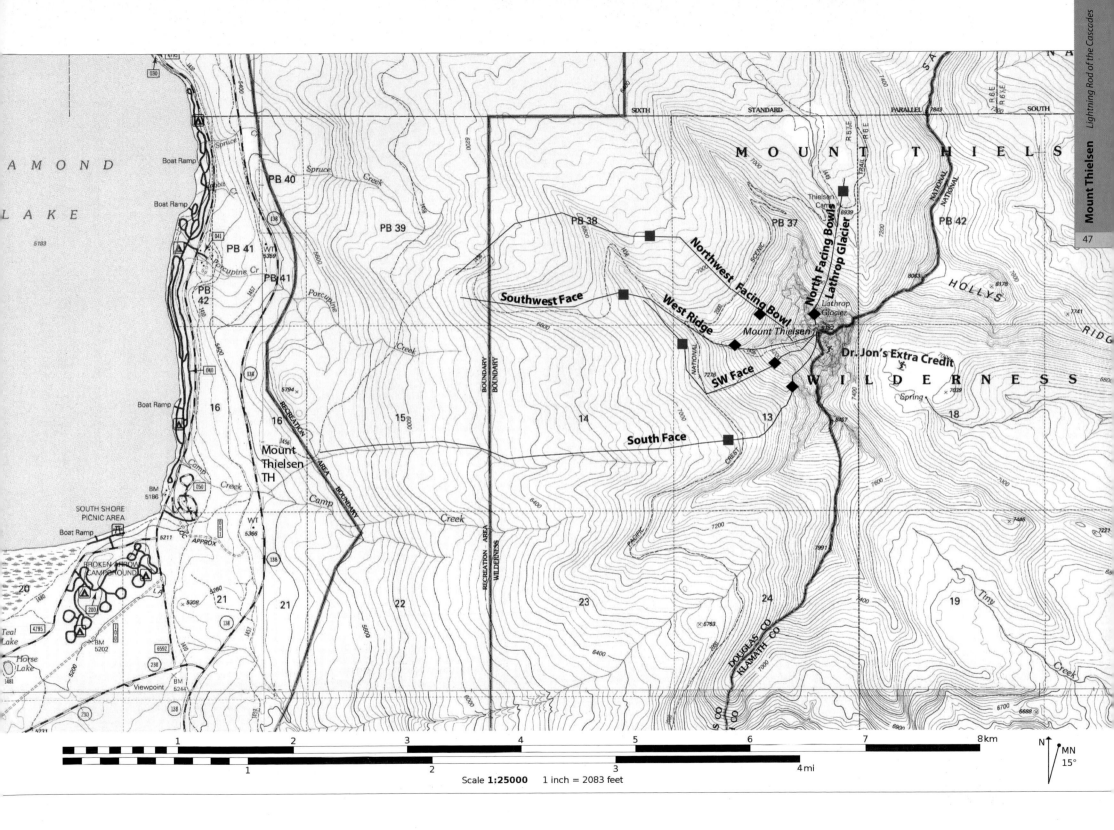

DIAMOND LAKE

MOUNT THIELSEN

HOLLYS RIDGE

WILDERNESS

Northwest Facing Bowl

North Facing Bowls

Lathrop Glacier

Southwest Face

West Ridge

SW Face

Mount Thielsen

Dr. Jon's Extra Credit

South Face

Mount Thielsen TH

PB 40
PB 39
PB 41
PB 41
PB 42
PB 38
PB 37
PB 42

BROKEN ARROW CAMPGROUND

SOUTH SHORE PICNIC AREA

Teal Lake

Horse Lake

Scale **1:25000**   1 inch = 2083 feet

0   1   2   3   4   5   6   7   8km

0   1   2   3   4mi

N   MN
15°

Diamond Peak

The Great Oregon Shield

8,744 ft | 2,665 m (43° 31' 15" N; 122° 08' 58" W)
Ski Descent May 11, 2014
First Ascent John Diamond and William Macy, 1852
First Ski Descent Unknown

Nearing the Corrigan Lake Trailhead in several inches of fresh snow.

Road Viewers Searching for the Lost Wagon Train of 1853

Three days of bad weather forced me to wait out the rain and snow in a nearby Oregon village to the southwest of Bend, Oregon. I was able to eat some solid meals and have some great rest knowing that high pressure would return to Oregon and I would likely be out again for several days in a row to climb these mighty volcanoes. Diamond Peak was the next volcano on my radar. Although Diamond is less than 9,000 feet high, it is easily Oregon's most isolated volcano, and relatively far from main roads and highways. The peak is a shield volcano that is broad and easily recognizable from most of the high peaks in central Oregon. I decided to access the peak from the southwest, which took me west from Diamond Lake over Emigrant Pass on Oregon Highway 58 to the small town of Oakridge. From there a very long road for 30 more miles (Rigdon Road #21), followed by a dirt and snow-covered Forest Service Road (2149), brought me to the snow line for mid-May at about 4,700 feet.

Basically I was in the middle of nowhere in the deep forests of Oregon. I can see why several hundred new settlers got lost in this area in the mid-1800s. John Diamond and William Macy climbed Diamond first in 1852 to scout out a potential route for their wagons and for the new emigrants. They took in views from McLoughlin to the south clear up to Jefferson to the north. Imagine if the two had skis back then and the fun that they could have had!

Skinning up near timberline in a winter wonderland on Mother's Day, 2014.

The Search for Oregon Blower Powder in May

I was excited to ski some Oregon powder when I parked my vehicle in 4 inches of fresh snow on the evening of May 10. I quickly prepared my daypack and went to bed early. Because I was delayed several days by the storm, my plan was to climb and ski Diamond in the morning and then head north to Mount Bachelor to spend the night on the top of Bachelor on the night of May 11th. It continued to rain and snow all night but I knew the forecast called for completely calm and clear conditions come the next morning, so I slept with confidence.

Sure enough, I awoke to bluebird skies on Mother's Day, May 11th, and I was off and skinning up the trees along the summer trail route for Diamond Peak and the Corrigan Lake Trail at first light. I followed a drainage for the first hour until the rising sun greeted me in some gladed trees and I caught my first glimpse of Diamond Peak to the north and east. It appeared to be a tall and broad significant mountain. The snow was deep and the clear blue skies and calm conditions beckoned me to timberline. I ascended a steep and sharp ridge that had a series of small rock pinnacles on it. For a short distance I put my skis on my back, eventually gaining a broad saddle on Diamond's western end at about 8,000 feet. The morning was incredibly calm and still cold. The sun's rays gave me strength and I pushed to the flat summit, finding myself all alone

at the top by 9:00 a.m. I had a bird's eye view of Thielsen, which kept my last bivy before the recent storm from that peak fresh in my mind.

In classic Colorado Fourteener bivy style, I broke out my bivy sack and took a short catnap in the morning sunshine. I also shot a couple of videos and in one I said hello and Happy Mother's Day to my mom because I didn't have cell phone coverage.

A Shield Volcano in the Rough of Central Oregon

Diamond Peak is huge because it is a broad shield volcano boasting two summits. The south summit is a bit higher and the entire peak is primarily composed of basaltic andesite. Many different ridges extend for a few miles in three directions. The large bowls and basins below the summit were likely cut from glaciers in the past several thousand years. I prepared myself to ski wishing I had several days here to explore each and every basin leading away from the top. Because Diamond Peak is farther west along the Pacific Crest in Oregon relative to the other volcanoes, the storms come off the Pacific and bury Diamond in deeper snow than most other locations.

Ski Descents and Potential Ski Lines

I clicked into my skis that morning and took full advantage of the fresh Oregon blower powder. There are so many different ways you could ski Diamond, but one thing to remember is that the volcano is extremely isolated. Get greedy and you could end up so far from your car and in the wrong drainage that you might end up lost like those emigrants long ago. Nevertheless, enjoy the stunning views and savor the fact that you've got at least 4,000 vertical feet to ski most years prior to June 1st.

The author pausing for a shot after skiing the upper west ridge/face of Diamond.

Dr. Jon's Recommendations

◆■ **Southwest Face and West Ridge/ Face** You'll likely climb the west ridge to get to the summit from Corrigan Lake. In safer avalanche conditions, take advantage of the southwest-facing bowl and enjoy a 35–40 degree slope down to treeline. If conditions aren't as safe as you'd like, follow the west ridge and your tracks back down to some easy slopes in a gentle bowl into the trees and back toward Corrigan Lake. If you choose the southwest face/bowl, remember to traverse to the west (skier's right) and around the southwest ridge to get back to your skin track and eventually the trailhead. (This route is about 4,000' vertical and 10 miles round-trip.)

◆ **Northwest Bowl** Ski these classic bowls directly from the summit if you like. There is a direct and very steep northwest line from the true summit and into the bowl. You can ski almost 2,500 vertical feet immediately to the trees. There are many choices in this bowl in all directions. You may get the feeling you are skiing something much bigger and in another part of the world when you are in these bowls. Once you are to timberline,

angle around the north side of the west sub-summit and north ridge of Point 8,306' to traverse out and back to the Corrigan Lake and Trailhead.

◆■ **South Ridge and Southeast Bowls** The ridge can be skied in extreme avalanche conditions and serves as probably the safest route on this peak. Lower-angled lines drop off of the ridge in a few places leading into a southeast-facing bowl. The Marie Lake Trailhead is the best option for this route, and the skiing is excellent from the summit directly south on the south face to Marie Lake and a gentle trail ski back to the Marie Lake Trailhead for a total of 3,600' vertical feet.

Dr Jon's Extra Credit: From the connecting saddle on the north ridge leading from Diamond's summit, take a skier's left and ski the **northwest ridge**, or right and to the **northeast faces**. It is possible to follow the **north ridge** and explore endless lines off the north aspect of the peak. You may want to consider using the access from Willamette Pass or even bring your overnight gear, as you'll be a long way out there on this one.

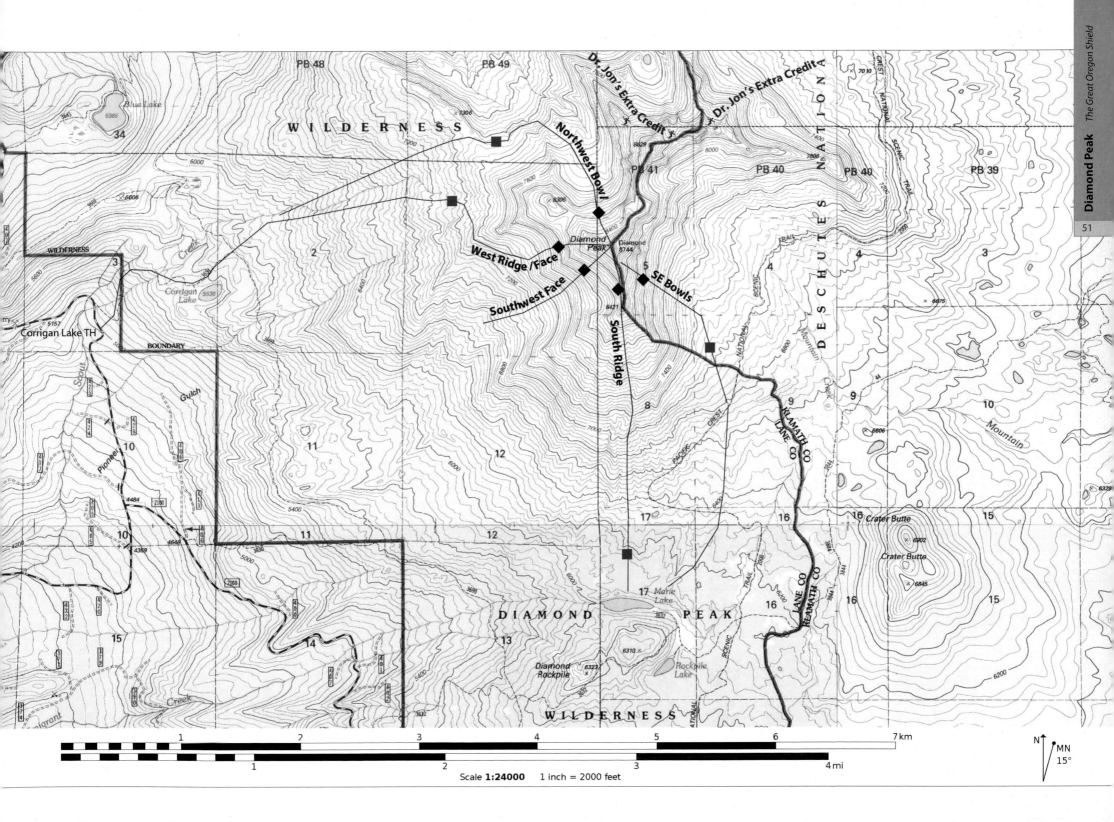

Scale **1:24000**   1 inch = 2000 feet

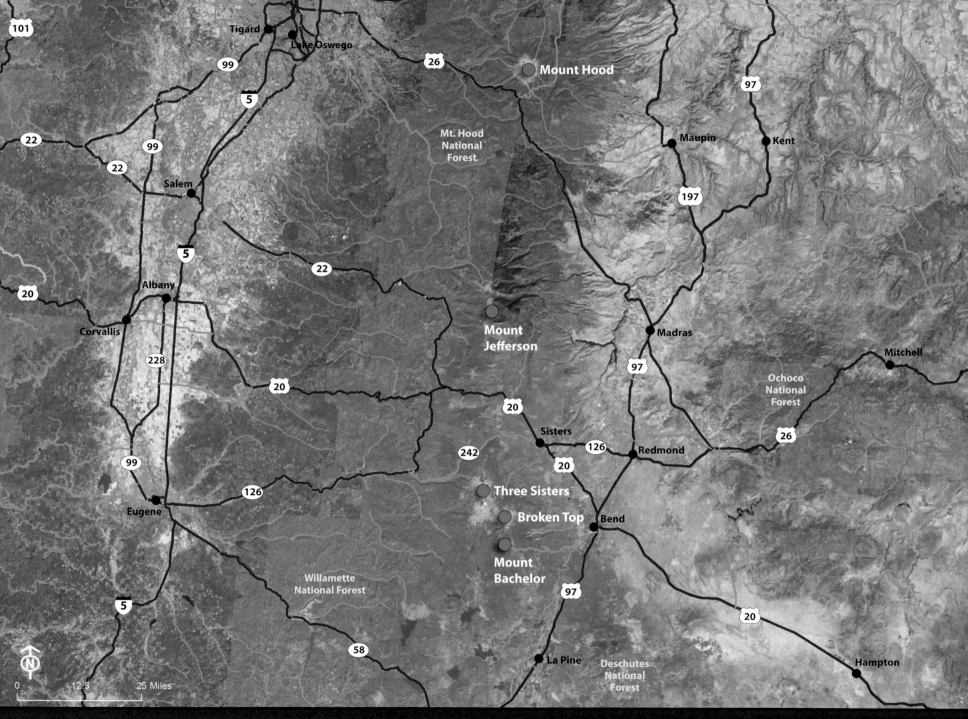

"My favorite part of skiing the volcanos of the Northwest is the juxtaposition of the various ecosystems you go through in just one day. You start amongst lush, green ferns and end up on these icy blue, crevassed covered summits. It's like two different worlds in one day, it's fantastic."

—**CHRISTY MAHON,** Ski Mountaineer

Sunrise on Mount Hood.
Upper right: The approach to Mount Jefferson.
Lower right: Colorful strata of Broken Top.

Mount Bachelor

Bachelor Butte—The Ski Resort Volcano

9,065 ft | 2,764 m (43° 58′ 46″ N; 121° 41′ 19″ W)
Bivy and Ski May 11–12, 2014
First Ascent Unknown
First Ski Descent Unknown; ski resort opened in 1958 by founder, Bill Healy

Mother's Day Journey

It was a very pleasant, warm spring day in central Oregon with temperatures in the sixties when I traveled several hours in my Tahoe to get from the base of Diamond Peak to the base of Mount Bachelor. My goal was to skin up Oregon's largest and most prominent ski resort, called Mount Bachelor, and spend the night on its summit. Upon arriving at the stratovolcano's base, I went from extremely isolated on the trip to being surrounded in a giant paved parking lot by campers, après skiers, and spring snow sports enthusiasts on the afternoon of May 11. "This might be an easy one," I said to myself, as I prepped my gear and got ready to skin up one of the ski trails en route to the top of the volcano.

The west face of Bachelor seen from Elk Lake.

I ate dinner in the parking lot around 4:00 p.m. and began my journey up the 2,800 vertical feet with simple overnight gear, two bottles of water, and some snacks for sunset as well as breakfast. I got to thinking about the journey so far. I was about halfway through with all my peaks on this adventure and enjoying every day on these giant Pacific Northwest volcanoes. There was an excellent high pressure weather window, providing amazing May weather, which would be in place for at least a week and maybe longer. Today's climb was about the same distance I always skin up, back home on Vail Mountain, from Lionshead to Eagle's Nest, when I'm home training. I simply took in the views as I got higher and higher and I thought about my mom. After all, it was her day. I thought about how important she and my dad were to me along with the rest of my family. Being safe on these volcanoes was mandatory, because there is always someone to go home to that cares about you. Before I knew it, I was making excellent time above the timber, along the west ridge and above to the high traverse, making my way onto the flat summit dome of the stratovolcano by 5:30 p.m., with plenty of time to get set up before the sunset.

Bachelor's Cinder Cone is visible from the northwest near Lake Todd.

The Great Helicopter Search-and-Rescue

I began to set up my tent on the top and took notice of a helicopter circling the mountain above me and all around the summit crater. Relaxing in light winds, I was also approached by a ski patrolman, who told me they were looking for a guy named Scott who got separated from his dad while skiing in the resort. I hadn't seen anyone matching the boy's description, but it got me thinking about my family again back home. Climbing mountains and skiing from their summits has become part of the fabric of who I am, but

Opposite: Sunset, South Sister seen in the distance.

Getting ready
to drop off the
summit.
Right: Not a bad
view to wake up
to, Three Sisters
in the distance.

no mountain or backcountry outing is worth dying for (or getting lost for). The evening wind gusted at times to 25 mph, but for the most part, I relaxed and enjoyed the evening and the sunset light reflecting on nearby Three Sisters and Broken Top to the northwest. It was very rewarding to look to the southwest and catch glimpses of Diamond Peak, which I had skied from that morning, about 75 miles away.

Mount Bachelor is properly named because it "stands alone," like a young bachelor. That evening I not only felt like a bachelor on that lofty summit—far from home and not involved in a significant relationship at the time—but I got to see that this project was truly standing alone from many of my previous accomplishments to date. Ten volcanoes down, ten to go. I slept soundly that night atop the volcano, which has rested in its dormant state for at least 10,000 years.

Sunrise to the Longest Birthday Ever

In the morning I woke up and the magnificent yellow light from the sunrise greeted me, and it occurred to me that it was my birthday. Looking over at the Three Sisters as well as at Broken Top, I knew that they were my next ski objectives. Many times you may be sitting on a particular summit along your path, an apex of success, but only for a moment. I could see the next four peaks I had to climb. They looked challenging, intimidating, huge! It was a long way to go, but the sooner I could pack up my tent and my gear and head toward them, the better my chances were to be successful. When you take in the views of your next mountain or mountains you have to climb, face the next challenge with the best of your ability and don't put it off: go for it as soon as you can. I was eager to step forward into the unknown and go after the next peaks whole-heartedly. After a hot drink on that summit, I packed up and skied down through the Mount Bachelor resort to my vehicle in less than thirty minutes. I would grab a morning breakfast burrito in one of the base restaurants and load up to head toward the Three Sisters. The birthday challenge was on!

Sunrise

Ski Descents and Potential Ski Lines

Mount Bachelor has unlimited ski potential. The ski resort takes up nearly all of the land on the volcano, and boasts the third (as of 2015) most lift-served skiable acres (3,683) for a single ski mountain in the United States. By 2016, the resort is looking to add a new lift from an approved 2013 Low East Catchment Line Expansion by the USFS Master Development Plan. One of the chairlifts (Summit Express) takes you to within a few hundred yards of the volcano's apex. It's quite common for people to take the short five- to ten-minute walk to the very top and then ski down the dozens of many ski trails dropping off the top in all directions. Climbing the peak without the aid of the chairlifts is steadily growing in popularity, so always check and abide by the Mount Bachelor uphill skiing policy, which can be found at: **http://www.mtbachelor.com/ site/winter/ski/uphill**. As of 2015, two of the safe and permitted uphill access trails and areas include the Cinder Cone Route and the East Side Summit Route. During some years, the west ridge to the high traverse is also permitted via the Cinder Cone access, but always check the status while planning your ascent.

Excellent view of the north ridge on Bachelor, which leads to groomed runs on the mountain.

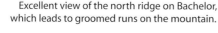

Lots of room on the summit to ponder your ski line while taking in the vistas.

Dr. Jon's Recommendations

Mount Bachelor Ski Resort trail maps available at: **http://www.mt bachelor.com/site/winter/ski/trail_map**. Officially, there are 88 named runs classified as: ● 15 percent Novice, ■ 25 percent Intermediate, ◆ 35 percent Advanced, ◆◆ 25 percent Expert

A Few Runs to Check Out on the Peak in the Resort

◆ **Osprey Way** A long fun run especially on a powder day. Use the Northwest Express on the back side of the mountain.

◆◆ **Northeast Cirque Bowl Options** Drop off the Hourglass directly off the north side of the summit. Prevailing westerly winds may also make the West Wall or Cliff Hanger especially epic.

■ ● **Healy Heights to Flying Dutchman to I-5** Blue/Green slopes accessed via the Summit Express chairlift make for an excellent Tour de Bachelor for nearly 3 miles. Great views toward Bend and the rest of eastern Oregon as you descend.

Dr Jon's Extra Credit: You could spend many days on a great ski vacation at the resort. Enjoy!

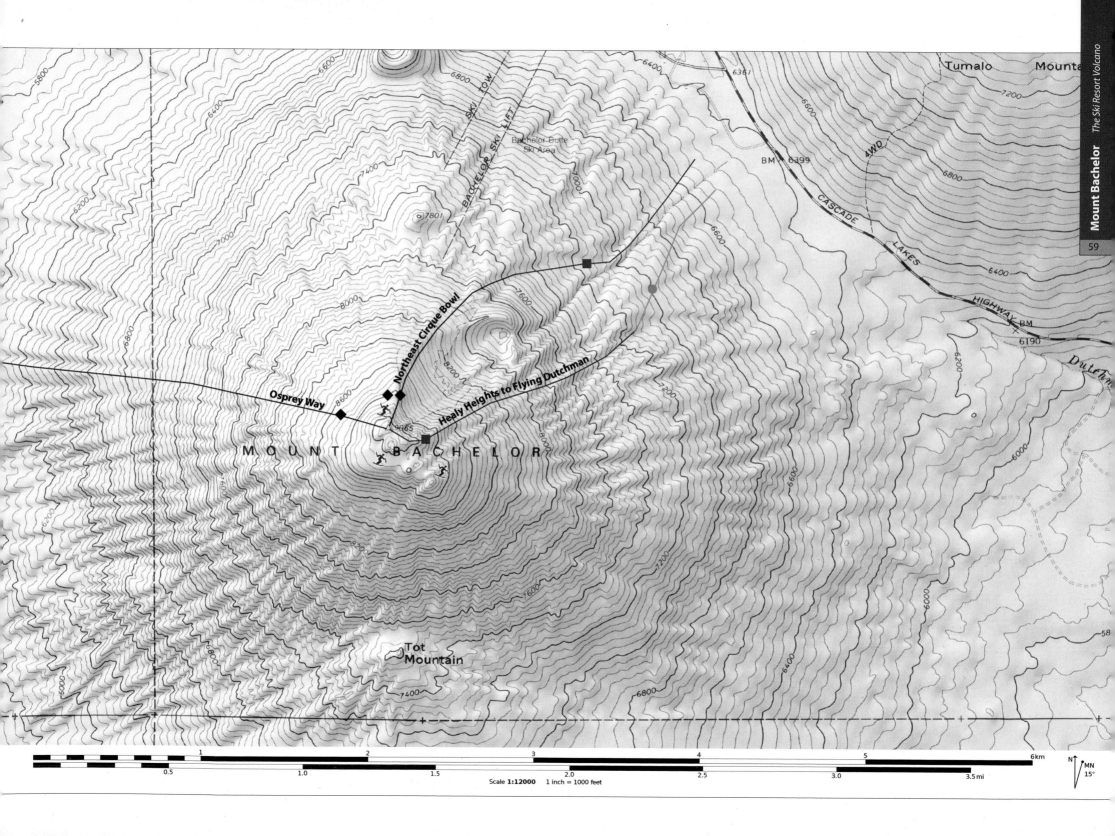

Tumalo Mountain

Bachelor Butte Ski Area

BM 6399

CASCADE LAKES

HIGHWAY BM 6190

Northeast Cirque Bowl

Osprey Way

Healy Heights to Flying Dutchman

M O U N T   B A C H E L O R

9065

Tot Mountain

Scale **1:12000**   1 inch = 1000 feet

THREE SISTERS

North Sister   Middle Sister

South Sister

Mount Bachelor

South Sister

Charity

10,358 ft | 3,157 m
(44° 06′ 12″ N; 121° 46′ 09″ W)
Bivy and Ski May 12–13, 2014
First Ascent Unknown
First Ski Descent Unknown

Approaching the Three Sisters the long way.

Longest Birthday Ever

When I finally crested the ridge of South Sister with the sun going down around 8:00 p.m. on the evening of May 12, I couldn't believe just how far I'd come. I had awakened that morning to catch the sunrise after spending the previous night on Mount Bachelor, over a dozen miles to the southeast. Bachelor's summit seemed light years away, and approaching the true summit of South Sister (10,358 ft), the third highest peak in Oregon, Bachelor looked like nothing but a small snow cone in the distance.

The entire day had been nice and sunny, and downright warm at times. When I got down from Bachelor that day I simply changed my clothes, treated myself to a birthday lunch burrito in the main ski lodge, repacked my food, and began the long ski to the Sisters group. Oregon Highway 46 was closed at the Mt. Bachelor Ski Resort because they only plow the road to the ski area in the winter. With no snowmobile or car as an option, and the road snowed in, I knew I would have to navigate carefully but make a strong push west for the day to make the top of South Sister.

The author pointing out the goal for sunset.
Right: The long crater rim with the small tent (left), and an eagle's eye view towards Middle and North Sisters.

Around 1:00 p.m. I started my journey. I traveled as light as I could with only my small tent, mini-stove, and a pot pie dehydrated meal for the night, as well as snacks for the entire trip. The goal was to bivy on the top of South Sister and then ski all three sisters to complete the "Three Sisters Marathon" the next day.

I started first on some rolling terrain through pine forests and open meadows. Broken Top, another volcano on my list for later in the week, stayed in my view as I traveled across the south flanks of the peak. Eventually I skied my way down a basin, carefully crossing some avalanche chutes to Green Lakes at about 7,000 feet. In the sweltering spring afternoon sun I still had a long way to go and time began to work against me. Five o'clock came and went. I skinned up the lower remnants of the Lewis Glacier, eventually meeting the South Sisters Trail, which was of course buried under snow. I didn't bring crampons to save on weight and the conditions were just right so that they weren't necessary. My ski boots plunged through the warm and softened snow for the last 500 feet up steep slopes to the crater rim. It was such an enjoyable day in the mountains of Oregon, and I felt so alone, but so excited about all this ski terrain that I had all to myself.

Summit camp just after sunrise. Below: The author on the summit of South Sister just in time for sunset.

Summit Crater also includes a feature called Teardrop Pool, the highest lake in Oregon, which stays buried under snow and ice most of the year.

Solitude and Wildness on the Dormant Giant Volcano

Once I reached the summit, I found a nice flat spot right on the northwestern side of the crater. Here I chopped out a quick platform for my tent and worked on getting my camp established while taking in a magnificent sunset and evening light show. The dramatic colors and fading cirrus clouds in the northern and eastern skies positioned themselves next to the pyramid shadow of the peak from the sun going down as the full moon rose to the east toward Bachelor. It was by far the calmest and most isolated summit I'd been on during this volcano tour. Even the dormant stratovolcano, the youngest but tallest of the Three Sisters, hadn't erupted for 2,000 years, so I felt like I was metaphorically camping with my sister who was deeply asleep. Tectonic uplift 3 miles west of the crater rim was discovered in 1997, and the area has seen some minor earthquakes and a measurable bulging of subsurface materials and magma up to 3 inches per year, which has slowed some since 2007.

But on that serene evening there didn't seem to be any volcanic activity to be concerned about. After enjoying the calm night, making my dinner, preparing my gear for the next day's ski tour, and rehydrating, I dozed off and slept soundly, truly a birthday I'll always remember—nearly 5,000 vertical feet of climbing and 14 miles of terrain after skiing down Bachelor—what a huge day!

There was absolutely no wind. It was by far the calmest bivy of this trip. South Sister, being my fifth overnight bivy of a volcano since May 1, was a real treat. I usually have to get bundled up and freeze my arse off in the wind when I take summit photos of the sunrises, but this one was dead calm. And I enjoyed every second of it.

Ski Descents and Potential Ski Lines

The amazing high-pressure weather gave me the opportunity to pursue the "Three Sisters Marathon" on May 13th. While I only skied one route off of the northeast face of South Sister, there are at least half a dozen classic ski lines, and maybe up to a dozen great ski routes off of South Sister. I chose the Prouty Glacier, via the steep and narrow Prouty Couloir. This ski line has a north to northeast aspect and is about 50 degrees. After skiing the first 1,000 feet down this narrow couloir, you exit the couloir by jumping a bergschrund crevasse at the head of Prouty Glacier and then the terrain opens up with some awesome turns down wide-open slopes to the saddle between South Sister and Middle Sister. I left the summit around 8:00 a.m. and the snow was already nice and soft. Then, after I exited the couloir to easier ground, the remaining 2,000 feet of vertical to the saddle between the two peaks was skied in a matter of minutes on perfect spring corn. The journey that day to ski the Sisters was well under way!

Prouty Couloir is steep and narrow before dropping onto the glacier.

Dr. Jon's Recommendations

Three of the best ski descents include:

◆ **Prouty Glacier** Drops off the northeast aspect, a classic 50-degee couloir at first from the eastern edge of the crater rim beginning north of Hodge Crest. After skiing the first thousand feet, the couloir ends and the slopes of the Prouty Glacier are wide open skiing northeast towards Carver Lake.

◆◆ **North Ridge Options** Includes the Silver Couloir, North Face Couloir, and Northwest Ridge, an alternative extreme way to ski north toward Middle Sister. A rappel may be required due to a distinct cliff band higher up.

■ ● **South Slopes** Gentle blue/green slopes below the initial headwall make for excellent sunny spring corn skiing. You have a choice of continuing back down in the direction of the South Sister Climbers Trail to Moraine Lake, or to the southeast on the **Lewis Glacier** and down to Green Lakes.

 Dr Jon's Extra Credit: These other climbing routes can offer great ski descents also: **West Ridge,** and the **East Ridge** via the **Old Crater Route** to Green Lakes.

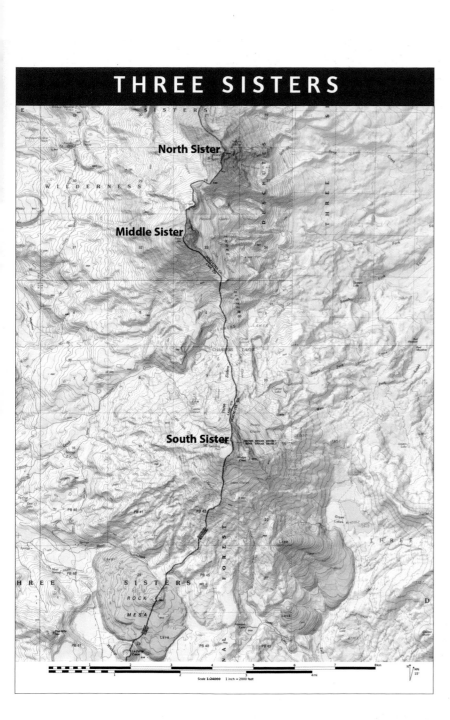

THREE SISTERS

North Sister

Middle Sister

South Sister

WILDERNESS

THREE SISTERS

NATIONAL FOREST

ROCK MESA

Lava

Scale 1:24000   1 inch = 2000 feet

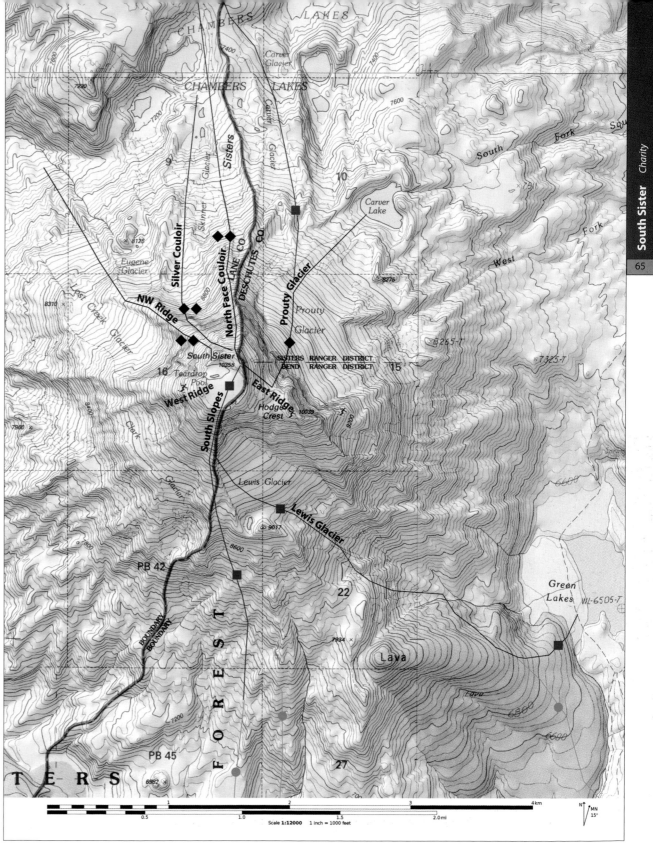

CHAMBERS   LAKES

Carver
Glacier

CHAMBERS   LAKES

Carver
Glacier

South Fork

Sisters

Skinner Glacier

Silver Couloir

North Face Couloir

NW Ridge

LANE CO.
DESCHUTES CO.

Prouty Glacier

Carver Lake

Prouty
Glacier

West   Fork

Eugene
Glacier

Lost Creek Glacier

South Sister
10358

SISTERS RANGER DISTRICT
BEND RANGER DISTRICT

Teardrop
Pool

West Ridge

South Slopes

East Ridge

Hodge
Crest   10039

Clark   Glacier

Glacier

Lewis Glacier

Lewis Glacier

PB 42

BOUNDARY
BOUNDARY

FOREST

Green
Lakes

WL-6505-T

Lava

PB 45

T E R S

Lava

Scale 1:12000   1 inch = 1000 feet

Middle Sister Hope

10,047 ft | 3,062 m (44° 07′ 04″ N; 121° 45′69″W)
Ski Descent May 13, 2014
First Ascent Unknown
First Ski Descent Unknown

The author's tracks in mid-afternoon after skiing Middle Sister (left), and North Sister (right). Right: Making fresh tracks from South Sister on the way to Middle Sister on the Prouty Glacier with Broken Top as a backdrop to the east.

Three Peaks in One Day

I remember how difficult yet how rewarding that day was when I skied all Three Sisters.

By 8:00 a.m., I had packed up and headed off the northeast flank of South Sister to a really amazing couloir, named the Prouty. It was kind of a hidden chute that provided passage to the valley below and a direct line to Middle Sister. Because it had only been about 48 hours since the last storm, the upper part of the chute was nice, soft, creamy powder; the lower part was faced into the morning sun but also skied very nicely.

Before I knew it I was speeding on my skis on a less steep volcanic basin on my way over to the base of Middle Sister. With heavy overnight gear, I knew that I would take too long, so I headed for the eastern flank of the Middle Sister at about 8,000 feet and took a break to cache some gear for the day.

Coming to a halt below Middle Sister's southeast ridge I looked behind me at South Sister. It felt surreal that I had been on the top of that giant only about an hour earlier. My ski of the Prouty Glacier and other glacially cut basins by the remnants of the Carver Glacier through the snow-covered Chambers Lakes had brought me now even farther away from my vehicle, which was way back at the base of the Bachelor Ski Area. Yesterday seemed like forever ago, and I certainly hoped that I would be able to make it back to my vehicle by nightfall.

The southeast ridge provides safe access to multiple ski lines on the peak. Here you can see the author's boot tracks on the ridge from earlier in the day and ski tracks from returning to pick up his gear cache.

From my vantage point, I could see North Sister and decided that doing these two peaks in a loop would be best. I could go up the southeast ridge to the south ridge of Middle Sister, and then traverse on the north ridge to North Sister and after topping out could ski the southeast face of North Sister. Then I would return back to my cached overnight gear, pick it up and begin the long 16-mile journey back to Mount Bachelor.

As I ascended the southeast ridge, the morning sun baked me like a chocolate chip cookie. Sweat poured down my face and I was getting dehydrated. I took the half-liter of water I carried and filled the bottle with snow and hung it on the outside of my pack in the sun. Buy the time I reached the summit, around 11:30 that morning, the snow had melted enough to provide a fresh drink for me. I repeated the process all day long as I didn't have any access to running water for the entire day and wouldn't drink anything bottled until I reached my truck that night.

Project Progress from the Perfectly Shaped Stratovolcano

Taking a break on Middle Sister's summit, I got to truly check my progress for the trip. I evaluated not only the situation for that day, but the situation for the project. I could see all the peaks I'd done looking to the south, and then I got to turn to the north and see just how much more I had left to do. All these mountains were truly metaphors for parts of life. Setting and accomplishing goals were all components of the journey. On Middle Sister I looked south to see Thielsen, Diamond, and Mount Bachelor, and looking north was North Sister, Jefferson, Hood, and Adams, plus more that were out of view. I felt great about the peaks I had summitted and skied, and I quietly celebrated some of my favorite moments from each peak as I saw them off in the distance. I also felt some excited apprehension about what was yet to come. Could I pull off my original plan to ski all of these giant volcanoes in the month of May? Heck, would I even be strong enough to make it up and over to North Sister and ski back out to the trailhead that day? I believed I could do it. Only time would tell, and it was time to get moving again.

I didn't have a moment to lose, so I clipped into my skis and dropped off the top of Middle Sister on an icy and powdery north ridge, with the Renfrew Glacier to the west. I eventually found myself at the saddle between Middle and North Sister at about 7,800 feet. To the west was Collier Glacier and to the east (right) was Hayden Glacier, so there was nowhere to go but up the south ridge/southwest face of North Sister from here. I may have been tired, but I still felt like I had one more climb left in me for the day.

Ski Descents and Potential Ski Lines

Middle Sister has at least six excellent ski options, and maybe more. While I was able to climb and ski the peak by linking all Three Sisters in a day, it's probably better to take advantage of this aesthetically beautiful volcano by packing in and camping somewhere in the basins to the east of the massive cirques making up Middle Sister's east faces. Some of the east-facing couloirs on Middle Sister are steep and glacially carved, while the north, west, and south sides provide slopes of 30–45 degrees and unlimited potential. The basin of the North Fork of Squaw Creek flows below the Diller Glacier. Choosing this for a basecamp and staying for a few days will allow you to explore not only the terrain of Middle Sister, but a couple of ski missions for North Sister are also nearby.

The east face of Middle Sister offers a couple of very narrow options that will drop you onto the Diller Glacier.

Dr. Jon's Recommendations

The best ski descents on Middle Sister include:

◆■ **Southeast Ridge/South Face** Drops off the south aspect of the peak. Variations include a direct line to the south face from the ridge, or just staying on the southeast ridge and skiing directly east toward the North Fork of Squaw Creek.

◆◆/◆ **North Ridge Options,** including the Northwest Face, Renfrew Glacier, and ■ Hayden Glacier. You can ski the north ridge for about 1,000 feet to access the Hayden Glacier at the Hayden-Renfrew Saddle, a prominent notch on the ridge.

◆◆ **Diller Glacier/East Face** A narrow 60–70-degree couloir that drops directly to the east below the southeast ridge about 400 feet below the summit. In a big snow year this chute is very direct and the snow will soften up before 9:00 a.m. because of the morning sun. It is best skied in May or June. Descend all the way back to the Pole Creek Trailhead for a 5,000-vertical-foot ski day.

Dr Jon's Extra Credit: The **east-facing cirque** of Middle Sister offers perhaps a few more technical ski lines such as the **northeast face** to Hayden Glacier direct, but approach with caution.

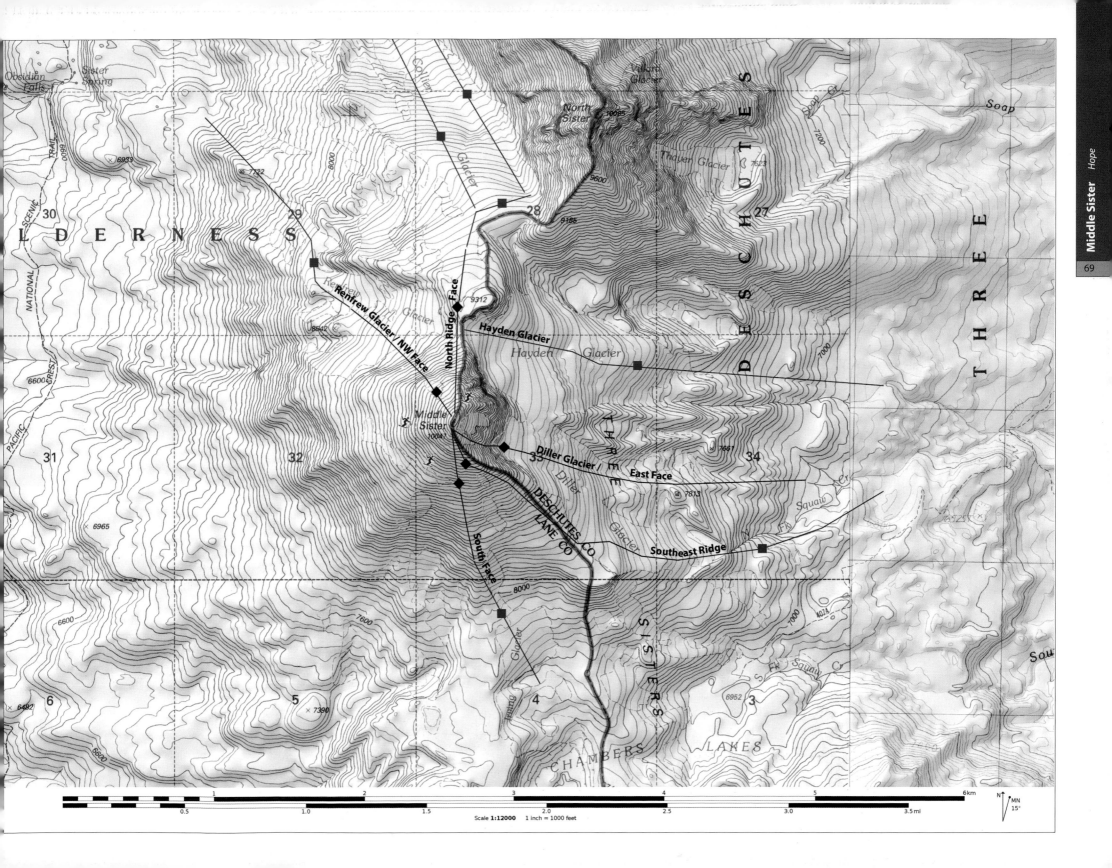

Renfrew Glacier / NW Face

North Ridge / Face

Hayden Glacier

Hayden   Glacier

Middle
Sister

Diller Glacier /   East Face

Southeast Ridge

South Face

DESCHUTES CO.
LANE CO.

Diller   Glacier

Hanging   Glacier

CHAMBERS   LAKES

SISTERS

THREE

DESCHUTES

WILDERNESS

North
Sister

Thayer Glacier

Villard
Glacier

Collier   Glacier

Renfrew   Glacier

PACIFIC   CREST   TRAIL

SCENIC   NATIONAL

Obsidian
Falls

Sister
Spring

Soap   Cr

N Fk Squaw   Cr

S Fk Squaw   Cr

Soap

Scale **1:12000**   1 inch = 1000 feet

N   MN
15°

North Sister

Faith

10,085 ft | 3,074 m (44° 07′ 23″ N; 121° 45′ 82″ W)
Ski Descent May 13, 2014
First Ascent Harley H. Prouty, 1910
First Ski Descent Unknown

The view from North Sister to the south is impressive. Views clear to Middle and South Sister, Broken Top (Left) and Mount Bachelor, as well as Diamond Peak on the far horizon.

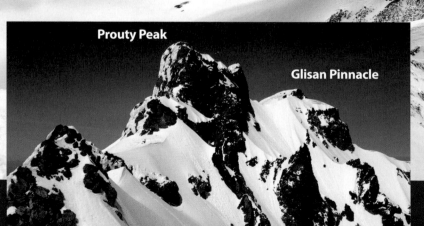

Prouty Peak

Glisan Pinnacle

A magnificent profile of North Sister while descending the north ridge of Middle Sister. Jefferson and Hood volcanoes are off in the distance. The west face ski lines are clearly visible on the peak.

Nothing to Lose and Everything to Gain

There was no wind all day and the heat was sweltering. I still had one more peak to do before I could get out of the wilderness. I had to dig deep. "Only a couple thousand feet to go, no biggie," I told myself. *Sometimes in life when you think you've got nothing more to give, yet you can still keep going, that's when you really make yourself better and stronger.* That day heading up North Sister was one of those days. I took a direct line up the southwest face until I met the south ridge partway up. There were a couple of guys coming off the summit by way of the "Terrible Traverse" to the west side of the peak, and they had left a backpack full of gear behind at the base of the ridge. Ravens had pecked through their stuff and it was all over the snow around me when I passed. I hoped that my gear I had left on the other side of Middle Sister earlier that morning had not succumbed to the same fate.

I passed the two guys who were descending when I reached the south ridge. I had been post-holing for several hundred feet on bad ice and snow on parts of the southwest face until I gained a much firmer ridge. The slope seemed pretty unstable to me. They were about 200 yards to my west still out on the southwest face, so I just waved goodbye and they wished me luck. "Be careful," they said, "conditions are getting soft." I could see that they did not like being out on that face. I certainly hoped that the slope would not avalanche as they made their way back down to the saddle and to their gear they had left behind. I heeded the warnings about things being soft and stayed on the crest of the ridge as I ascended.

The South Ridge of North Sister puts you in a great position to make the final ascent to the Camel's Hump and Prouty Peak.

Bowling Alley of Loose Rock, But Not in Snowy Conditions

A shallow gully later and I was standing on the Camel's Hump, a prominent feature just to the south of the true summit, called Prouty Horn. North Sister is the oldest and most eroded volcano of the Three Sisters. It has been extinct for 100,000 years as a stratovolcano atop an ancient shield volcano called Little Brother. Rockfall was a constant concern of mine, but since the peak was pretty well snow-covered, the basaltic andesite and palagonite red and black cinder boulders were not a factor. I crossed the "Terrible Traverse" and booted my way up a steep couloir of sorts through the "Prouty Horns." The summit was so snow-covered that I didn't have to climb on any rock to tag the true summit. The views were impressive and making it to the top of the third Sister was a real reward!

Once I skied safely back down to the Camel's Hump from off the summit, I knew I had this one in the bag. The time was 1:00 p.m. I made quick turns down the south face, crossed the Hayden Glacier, slogged back across the Diller Glacier, and found my gear safely cached where I had left it.

After a brief lunch I had to keep going. No less than 16 miles separated me from the safety of my vehicle near Mount Bachelor. Exhausted, dehydrated, and over-heated from the amazing stable day in Oregon, I arrived in darkness back at the trailhead at 10:00 p.m. I could hardly believe that I skied all Three Sisters in a day! But there was still more to do.

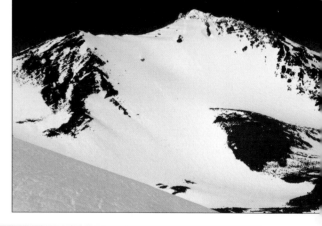

The South Slopes offers a wide open skiing experience.

Ski Descents and Potential Ski Lines

North Sister has at least four excellent ski options, and this volcano is one of the most technical to ski of any in the entire Pacific Northwest. It is by far the most difficult peak to ski out of the Three Sisters. You can drop directly off the summit pinnacle of Prouty Peak or even Glisan Pinnacle to reach the four ski lines mentioned here if the cornices are large enough and solid. Take advantage of stable conditions in May or June and this peak can be very rewarding.

Dr. Jon's Recommendations

When skiing the west and south aspects of North Sister (#1 and #2 below), use the Obsidian Trailhead (3528A) off of Oregon Highway 242 to the southwest of McKenzie Pass. Eastern and northern aspects of the peak (#3 and #4) can be accessed from Pole Creek Springs Trailhead (96D) at the end of Forest Road 1018 to Forest Road 1524, also off Oregon Highway 242 at McKenzie Pass. The best ski descents on North Sister include:

◆◆/◆ **1. Southeast Ridge/South Face** The best ski line begins directly off of the Camel's Hump. After skiing the chute through the Prouty Horns across the Terrible Traverse and booting back atop Camel's Hump, choose a narrow gully that initially keeps you on the ridge or just to the south of the southeast ridge. The south face then opens up nicely for pure corn turns for several hundred feet into the Hayden Glacier Basin.

◆◆/◆ **2. South Ridge/West Face Options** You can get to the west face's southwestern variations by choosing one of the narrow chutes immediately below the Terrible Traverse on the west face. Alternatively, you can take the same line as in option #1 above to reach the Camel's Hump. Dropping off the Camel's Hump, to skier's right, select from a pair of gullies that allow you to ski down the west face directly. Choose the best line based on what you see and assess on your ascent, finishing near the saddle between the Collier-Hayden Col and Glaciers. ■ The Collier Glacier, the largest glacier in Oregon by surface area, extends this route toward the west and back toward the Obsidian Trailhead.

◆◆/◆ **3. Early Morning Couloir** A narrow and funneling 50–60-degree couloir that drops directly to the east/northeast down a gully to skier's right from the Glisan Pinnacle. This line is classic and very direct. The snow will soften up early, so ski before 10:00 a.m. because of the morning sun. It is best skied in May or June, but is skiable into July some seasons. Descend all the way back to the Pole Creek Springs Trailhead.

◆◆/◆ **4. Villard Face and Glacier** Although not quite as steep or aesthetic as the Early Morning Couloir, the entire northeast face of North Sister is a great ski. Instead of taking skier's right into the Early Morning Couloir, look to skier's left once you have cleared the base of the Glisan Pinnacle. Once through the initial narrow section, the face opens up and provides over a thousand feet of pure corn turns in the morning sunshine. Access this line by way of the Pole Creek Springs TH, Three Sisters Trail 96, and Soap Creek.

Dr Jon's Extra Credit: The terrain spanning the **northwest arête to the northwest ridge** extending north down to the remnants of the **Linn Glacier** may be worth the extra effort. Skiing the east arête from Glisan Pinnacle and dropping to the south then east onto **Thayer Glacier** would also be an exciting descent.

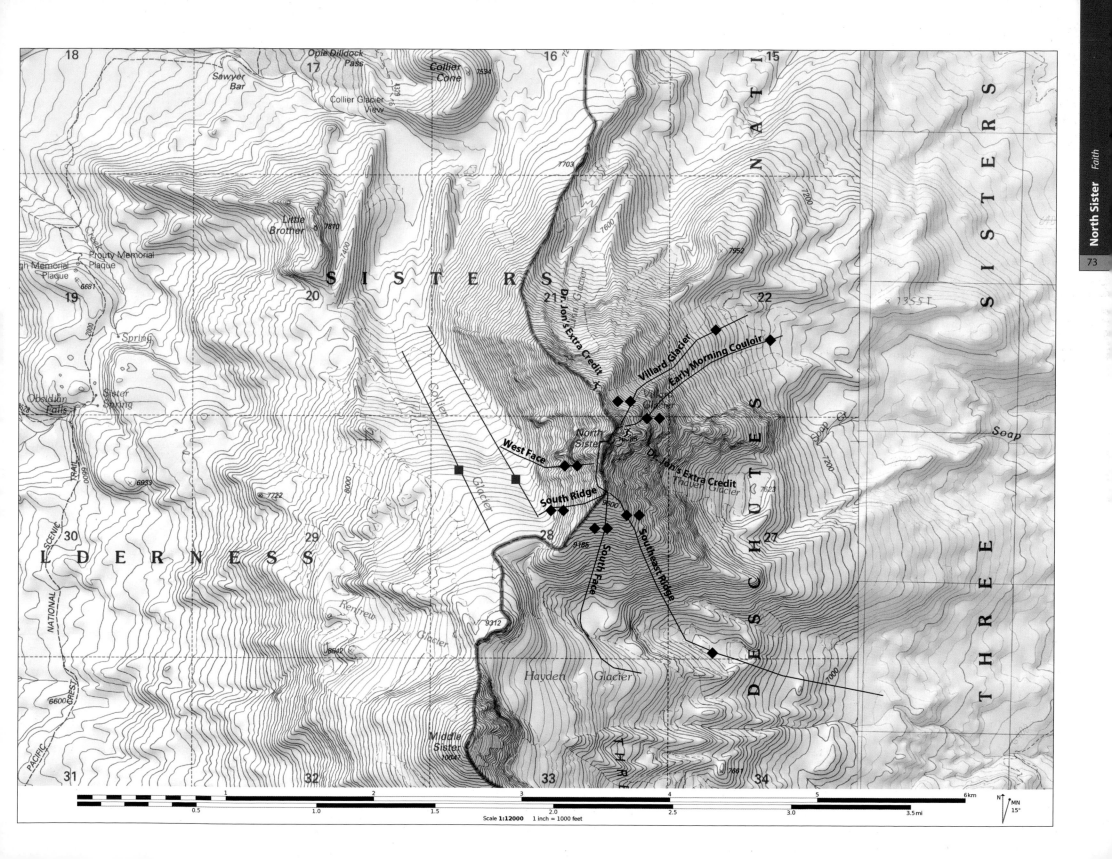

Broken Top

The Nine and Eleven O'Clock Couloirs

9,175 ft | 2,797 m (44° 04′ 58″ N; 121° 41′ 59″ W)
Ski Descent May 15, 2014
First Ascent Unknown
First Ski Descent Unknown

There are many jagged points along Broken Top, and skiing the peak from the south allows you to explore the crater of the volcano and actually climb out of the center by one of many couloirs.

Broken Top *The Nine and Eleven O'Clock Couloirs*

75

Oregon's Deep World of Volcanoes

Broken Top was all that remained in the immediate area that I still wanted to ski. I had one more peak to do before I would head north to Hood and Jefferson. After the exhausting day finishing off the Three Sisters, I spent the following day (May 14) in nearby Bend, Oregon, exploring the town, catching up on writing, and eating and drinking as much as I could put down. This central Oregon region holds the most concentrated landscape of volcanoes in the Pacific Northwest, and while standing in Bend on an 80-degree May day, the western skyline was dominated by Bachelor, Three Sisters, and Broken Top. Of these volcanoes, Broken Top is appropriately named, as it literally looks like the volcano blew its top leaving nothing but a large crater and some giant walls and steep ridges to guard a very small and sharp summit. In summer after the snow melts, a crater east of the volcano boasts one of the most spectacular lakes in all of America, a hidden gem known as "No Name Lake." When looking at the volcano from the vicinity of Mount Bachelor, I was excited to get to ski into the exposed cone of the peak, be near the frozen snow-covered lake, and then choose one of its steep couloirs to climb. From the city, I envisioned myself solving the puzzle to the top by scrambling a ridge and finding my way to a small summit. I was looking forward to seeing what sort of ski terrain I would find. I planned to start early after getting to bed in the back of my Tahoe at the trailhead on the evening of May 14th.

A view down into the crater and back towards Mount Bachelor.

Opposite: The highest point on Broken Top is small and rocky with an excellent perspective towards northern Oregon.

Importance of Starting Early

I slept in until 6:00 a.m. on the morning of May 15th. I originally planned to leave the trailhead at 4:00 a.m. so that I would be climbing frozen snow on the peak and not concerned about wet avalanches on both my ascent and ski decent. But the previous weeks were starting to catch up with me. I made the most of my start and got going at 6:30 a.m. I was definitely ready to head north in Oregon and to some new peaks, but I still had to push through this one.

My same route, through relatively flat meadows and pine trees, from two days before, was used to gain the wilderness boundary as I traveled from Mount Bachelor toward the southeast facing bowl of Broken Top. The volcano beckoned me as the morning sun shone on its giant walls. Around 8:00 a.m. I took a right turn up a basin leading to the peak. The giant crater began swallowing me up as I skinned onto the Crook Glacier. No wind once again that morning so I was down to one layer and melting away in the heat. Two prominent and steep couloirs, appropriately named "Nine O'Clock" and "Eleven O'Clock" due to their orientation, revealed the most obvious escape out of the crater bowl that I was in on the Crook Glacier.

Right at 9:00 a.m., I decided to take the namesake couloir. It was so warm as I stepped upwards on a 50-degree slope that I sank into slushy snow up to my knees. "I shoulda started earlier." The western wall of the couloir was getting baked. Fortunately in a few more steps the snow firmed up enough, but I was still concerned. I got into a quick rhythm, and went as hard and fast as I could up the chute. At the top there was a 10-foot cornice I had to climb straight over, and that was the toughest part. Using the rock to the right of the top of the couloir, I gently stepped over the cornice, and when I finally made it to the flat saddle, I peered down the gully I had just ascended with relief. "Next time start earlier," I told myself.

As the sun heats up the snow it gains weight and can collapse and slide. The water acts as a lubricant and large wet slabs can release and are quite dangerous. Fortunately it was still early, but I had to climb fast up the ridge to the top and I would try my luck skiing a different couloir on the descent. Not only do the names of these couloirs represent their orientations relative to the clock on the wall, but they likely indicate the latest hour of the morning that you should probably be climbing up and skiing down them.

Summit Block Geology and Skiability

In the summer, the final 150 feet of the peak is guarded by a large rock band of andesite lava that you have to climb, but that day on Broken Top, I searched to the north side of the summit block and found a perfect 50-degree snow wall to climb, which allowed me safe and instant access to the true summit. By 10:30 a.m. I was hanging out with an impressive view and a newly climbed volcano, my thirteenth peak in fifteen days. I couldn't wait to click into my skis and ski directly off the top!

Due to extensive erosion, Broken Top's cone is exposed, making it a complex stratovolcano. The rocks making up the crater walls consist of andesite, dacite, rhyodacite, and pyroclastic flows that have been dormant for at least the past 100,000 years. Expect Broken Top to continue to erode and break away over the next several thousand years.

Ski Descents and Potential Ski Lines

Broken Top is one of the most underrated skiing peaks in the Pacific Northwest because it is overshadowed by Mount Bachelor and the Three Sisters. With only Jefferson and Hood remaining for me to ski in Oregon, I was eager to make it down multiple slope aspects of Broken Top, which has some great steep ski lines on it. Not only is the peak accessed from Mount Bachelor, but western lines on the face of Broken Top south of the northwest ridge can be skied down to Green Lakes at the base of South Sister. The north side of the summit can be skied directly off the top if there is enough snow, as a perfect 50-degree snow wall exists to climb and also to descend.

The author christened this final pitch to the summit the "North K" Couloir because the right amount of snow allows a steep snow climb combined with some perfect turns to get back to the base of the tower.

Dr. Jon's Recommendations

When skiing routes leading into the crater bowl, onto the Crook Glacier, or towards No Name Lake, Broken Top can be accessed in winter from parking at the Mount Bachelor Ski Area. In the spring and early summer, by mid-May, you can start from above Todd Lake by driving Oregon 46 to Forest Road 370 and parking on the end of Forest Road 380. For west face access, use the Green Lakes Trailhead off of Oregon 46. Broken Top's best ski descents include:

◆◆/◆ **Eleven O'Clock Couloir** This classic couloir is a must-ski option on Broken Top. After skiing the "North K Couloir" for 150 feet off the summit, make a left U-turn and traverse south along the top of the west face for a couple hundred yards until you reach a flat notch. From the notch you can stand atop a solid cornice and peer down the Eleven O-Clock Couloir. From March until mid-June, this 50-degree chute is the finest line into the crater on Broken Top. The chute starts quite narrow but opens up into a broad crater face where you can carve solid turns onto the Crook Glacier and ski out the basin to the trailhead near Todd Lake or back to Mount Bachelor. On warmer spring days, be aware that the sun will bake this chute, making wet avalanches a concern. I definitely would ski it well before 11:00 a.m. if you can! This trip is 3,000 feet of vertical climbing/skiing and 11 miles round-trip.

◆◆/◆ **Nine O'Clock Couloir** The Nine O'Clock Couloir is shorter, steeper, and narrower than the Eleven O'Clock Couloir. Make sure you climb this chute well before 9:00 a.m. so that you can ski it before the sun softens it up too much. Dropping off the north side of the summit, follow the same route as above to reach the top of the Eleven O'Clock Couloir, then traverse for another 200 yards again to the south above the west face to reach the notch that begins the Nine O-Clock Couloir.

◆ **West Face** Once off the initial summit of "North K Couloir," turn left and work your way out onto the broad west face. This face has a pair of broad and wide-open slopes that ski 35–45 degrees for a sustained 2,000 feet. Once back to timberline, follow open glades and more relaxing treed slopes back to the vicinity of Green Lakes.

◆ **South Gully** This ski line drops directly into the crater from a broad gap in the crater rim. The north side of the rim, for a quarter mile, coming down from the summit to the broad gap, is usually difficult to navigate on skis, but skiing down into the crater to the Crook Glacier from the rim is an outstanding line heading south and then east (skier's right).

Dr Jon's Extra Credit: Two extreme ski lines that may also include some rappelling are the **north face** of Broken Top down to **Bend Glacier,** and the **"High Noon Direct,"** which follows cliffs directly south off the summit into the crater and onto steep snow slopes onto Crook Glacier below. If you are later in the summer season and have time, visiting **No Name Lake** is an opportunity you won't want to miss.

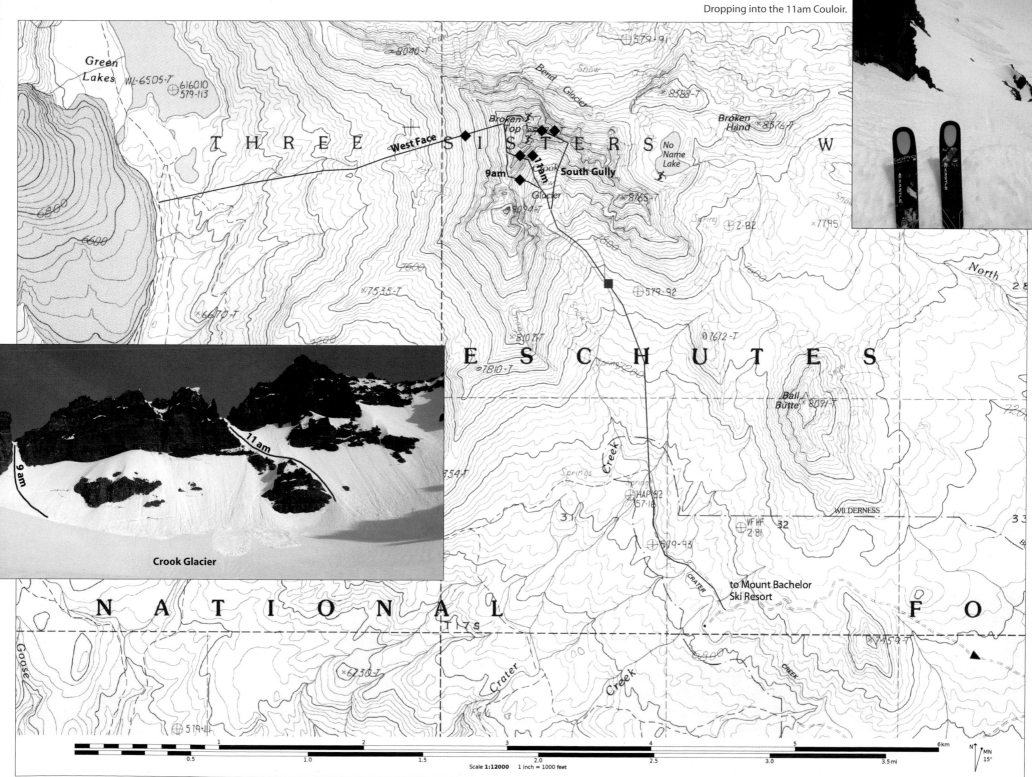

Dropping into the 11am Couloir.

Green Lakes

WL-6505-T
⊕ 616010
579-113

THREE   SISTERS

West Face

Broken Top

Bend Glacier

Broken Hand × 8576-T

No Name Lake

9am

11am   South Gully

Crook Glacier

DESCHUTES

Ball Butte × 8091-T

9 am

11 am

Crook Glacier

Creek

Springs

to Mount Bachelor Ski Resort

WILDERNESS

NATIONAL   FO

Scale 1:12000   1 inch = 1000 feet

N
MN
15°

Mount Hood

Wy'east

11,239 ft | 3,426 m (45° 22' 25" N; 121° 41'45" W)
Bivy and Ski May 16–17, 2014
First Ascent Henry L. Pittock, W. Lymen Chittenden,
Wilbur Cornell, Prof. L.J. Lowell, William S. Buckley,
James G. Deardorff, and Rev. T.A. Wood, July 11, 1857
First Ski Descent Andre Roch, Hjalmar Hvam, and
Arne Stene, who skied most of the peak, 1931; Sylvain
Saudan (from true summit), 1971

Highest Peak in Oregon

After finishing off Broken Top with an excellent ski descent, I headed north and west toward Portland, Oregon. My good friend Mike Lewis was planning on flying into Portland to join me on a couple of peaks, so I had to pick him up. As I passed Timberline Lodge and drove past the mighty Mount Hood on my way to Portland International Airport, I feasted my eyes on the prize. "I'll be back tomorrow," I said, as I glanced out the window at the icy snow-clad beast of a peak and headed for the city. Mike was flying in the next morning and we would head up to Hood to try and attempt a summit bivy the next evening.

A pair of skiers make their way up towards Crater Rock.

Right: Chopping platforms into the side of the cornice provided little protection against the winds as the clouds moved in for sunset.

Opposite: Our two tents were certainly the highest campsite in Oregon for that evening.

Threading the Needle to Stitch a Summit Bivy and Descent on Hood

Mike was in good spirits as he came out to see what this "Sleeping on the Summits" and skiing project (or split-boarding in his case) was all about. We knew that a storm was coming in on the morning of the 17th, so we decided to climb on the 16th and would pack up as early as possible from the summit to come down to the friendly accommodations of the famous Timberline Lodge. With full packs, we departed the parking lot at the lodge and the base of the ski area at 1:00 p.m., plenty of time to climb the vertical mile (5,280 feet) and make a summit camp by sunset.

While we ascended the Palmer Glacier, the packs started to get heavy, but we forged on. Winds stayed light, and we both knew about the approaching storm for the morning as well as some of the notoriously documented and media sensationalized accidents from the mountain in recent years, many due to the weather turning bad. If you do decide to climb Mount Hood, start early and turn back immediately if conditions deteriorate. Our goal was to not become another statistic. As we climbed past Crater Rock and up into the crater, the peak itself seemed to be blocking the westerly winds. Once we made the Hogsback, we could tell the standard "Pearly Gates" route was a no-go as the bergschrund crevasse guarding it was too large (see photo page 81). So we headed up the "Old Crater Route."

The time was 5:00 p.m. so Mike gave me the okay to push ahead so that I could get up to the summit and start chopping out platforms for our tents. Once I climbed a small icy chute, I stood on the west summit ridge and was almost blown away as my skis acted as wind-sails! The strong winds would be an issue on the summit, so I carefully strolled over to the top and found a relatively protected spot with room enough for two tents and a cornice providing some wind blockage and began digging in and chopping us out some platforms.

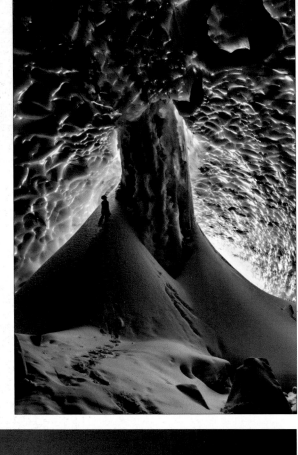

Famous Oregon Volcano is Still Semi-Active

Once Mike arrived, we finished up the platforms, secured our tents in the 40 mph gusts, and made some hot drinks and dinner. The drop-off on the north side of Hood is fatally steep, so we kept reminding each other not to walk too close to the edge. The smell of sulfur in the air all night long was nauseating. Geologists note that while Mount Hood is not currently active, there is a slight chance that there could be minor eruptions from these relatively active vents, which could cause significant mudflows, lahars, and avalanches on the mountain within the next century. The last notable eruptive activity was over a hundred years ago in 1907. In addition, if you decide to climb Mount Hood, the fumarole vents are a hazard not only for people that have fallen into them, but for the sulfur dioxide gasses, which are poisonous and have claimed several lives over the years. Stay clear of these openings in the glacier and near the Old Crater so that you don't become the next victim.

Left: Stacia Glenn stares in wonder at the largest ice formation in Pure Imagination. Constant debris fall makes the caves dangerous to enter but winter is the safest time because the ice melts slower and fewer rocks tumble from the ceiling and walls. Photo by Aaron Frank.

The sulfur vents are exposed on the way to the summit along the Hogsback route; the smell reminds you of the volcanic activity here.

Right: Aaron Frank stands in the middle of Snow Dragon, the largest of three ice caves discovered on the west side of Mount Hood in 2011. An unseasonably warm winter led to a partial collapse of the cave in 2015. Photo by Stacia Glenn.

A Split-Boarder's Perspective

Dr. Jon Kedrowski is a man with ideas as grandiose as the peaks he parlays into unique experiences through lenses all his own, lenses that have shifted their gaze to the wilds of the California 14ers and the volcanoes of the Cascades that form the northeast rim of the Ring of Fire in a legendary land of Pacific Northwest lore.

Perhaps nowhere is this lore more ensconced than on the shoulders of northern Oregon's Mt. Hood, the sentinel standing guard over Portland, a mountain that helped forge America's love affair with skiing and served as a springboard and cause de célèbre for pushing the country past the depression with the construction of the WPA and CCC's Timberline Lodge.

But yet again we get ahead of ourselves.

Over lunch in early spring as Kedrowski outlined his plans for his #Sleeping OnTheSummits2 Tour, hastily-made plans for us to unite in mid-May were laid. The sort of commitment you craft out of civility, then gained possibility and weight as Kedrowski's tour unfolded, with one peak after another on his northerly journey playing host to his high-country bivy. The images and tales rolled in, forcing an inevitability to joining him—to see for ourselves what so inspired him about experiencing these mountains differently.

And so for several days leading up to our departure we hastily gathered the necessities of camping in a place where no person is meant to live. A place that claimed the life of Father Robert J. Cormier on May 13, who tumbled 1,000 feet down the north face of the mountain after summiting solo ahead of his group. A fact that gave us pause and focus as we gathered crampons, ice axes, and dehydrated meals.

The mission began to truly take focus through blurry, lidded eyes as the alarm broke the fog of sleep at 3:00 a.m. on May 16. Feet trudged methodically through motions to a packed car, to DIA, with eyes re-opening at PDX. Swooped up by the rolling lodge of a Chevy Tahoe that has become Kedrowski's intermittent home between summit pushes and onwards to the parking lot of the Timberline Lodge.

Used to the downward pull of gravity through the courtesy of chairlifts, the upward push on the flanks of Timberline's slopes, still blanketed with the massive sculptures of freestyle progression that is Snowboarder's Superpark, felt like a trip through the looking glass.

Reflecting on how ideas of fun and human progression evolve over a lifetime, we trudged ever upwards on the low angle terrain, fodder for younger versions of ourselves to spray with snow and wonder what in the hell would compel a person to forsake a perfectly good chairlift to slog upwards when perfect jumps await mere yards away.

But onwards we trekked and gradually the angle began to lift under our feet, and as we peeled our eyes from the drudgery directly beneath us, the landscape unfolded into a detail that from even the top of the Palmer Lift seems impossible.

The crater greeted us with its sulfurous stench, the smell of impending victory and wariness as bergschrunds yawned above and fumaroles and crevasses gaped below. The pitch began in earnest up the side of the crater that began forming more than half a million years ago, as the Juan de Fuca plate slid slowly under the Pacific Northwest, blasting its top at interludes, shaping the countryside around it, with its last major top-popping morphology shaking the land in the 1790s, shortly before the arrival of Lewis and Clark.

With the classic route of the Pearly Gates blocked by a gaping bergschund more than 100 feet wide, as the uppermost section of the White River Glacier peeled itself off at the top of the Hogsback in just the last week, we skirted around the West Crater Rim, reaching the wind-tattered summit at 11,239 feet at 7:30 p.m., just as the magic hour started to descend along with the thermometer.

An old hand at assessing safe purchase, Kedrowski immediately began to dig in, carving a platform out of a leeward slope just yards from the perilous north face which had claimed the life of the 57-year-old Cormier just three days prior. With furious ice axe and Snow Claw slashes, a landing pad for two tents emerged, dry clothes were greeted, and camera equipment emerged. A cloud bank rolled in seemingly on cue, bringing fire to a sunset that seemed to erupt below the sputtering volcano as far as the eye could see, bringing to life and light one of the most truly magical sunsets eyes ever beheld.

With light hearts and heavy muscles we retreated to our tents and the embrace of down bags packed full of gloves, water, boot liners, and everything we needed to protect from the freezing winds of our substandard two-season tent, whose rain fly welcomed the elements leaving but a screen between us and the stars through the night.

With earplugs and a zero-degree bag slowly bringing the embrace of sleep, dawn broke with equally energetic fire a few short hours later and the Saturday morning train of climbers began to crest the crater rim as eager expectations of being the day's first to summit were shattered by the sight of our tents and a fast-moving cloud break made for a short-lived time on the peak and near zero visibility.

And so our time atop this sentinel came to a close as well, with hurried, measured crampons clomping down the upper regions, before smoother snows greeted the hungry edges of our skis and snowboards on the lower reaches of the Hogsback, ushering us down by the grace of gravity to the smoother slopes of the gloriously groomed Palmer Snowfield at 8,540', and the beckoning embrace of the Timberline Lodge's magical buffet, hot tub, history, and creature comforts—just over an hour below, yet an impossible distance away from the summit of Mt. Hood.

—Mike Lewis

Storm Rolling in at Sunset

There was a lower cloud deck coming in from the Pacific Ocean as the sun went down. The clouds started to surround the peak, and many of the twelve glaciers on all sides of us down the mountain were becoming obscured as we enjoyed the awesome colors and light show above the cloud deck. St. Helens, Adams, and Rainier to the west and north, and Jefferson to the south, all stayed above the clouds. Winds remained strong all night, but because we were only at 11,239 feet, I ended up sleeping well with earplugs. We woke to more clouds rolling in and a threatening storm along with strong winds. Right at sunrise, just before 5:30 a.m., the contrast of clouds and sunlight was very impressive. When Mike emerged from his tent, we both knew what was coming. We packed up as fast as we could and started our descent. We unfortunately had to take icy conditions and lack of spring corn over the fact that we didn't want to get trapped in that oncoming storm. This all made the vertical mile we skied that morning very bittersweet, but knowing we would be back to the Timberline Lodge in less than an hour, we moved quickly. We carefully navigated the icy Old Crater on descent, and were carving turns down the Palmer Glacier in increasing snow flurries. By 9:30 a.m. we had checked into the Timberline Lodge and were soaking up our awesome success on Hood in the hot tub. Meanwhile, the mountain was engulfed in a lenticular cloud and the snow intensified. We had spent the night on Hood and skied down safely!

Ski Descents and Potential Ski Lines

Mount Hood is a sought-after stratovolcano and a relatively steep cone. A minimum of six stellar ski lines drop directly from the true summit in all directions. Until the initial steepness is navigated from near the summit, upon descent of nearly every route, the potential for dangerous conditions, exposed ski lines, and icy/rocky terrain exists. Skiing Mount Hood is not for beginning ski mountaineers. The routes directly off the summit can be very narrow, steep, and dangerous. Lower down on the mountain, however, there is lots of skiing to be had. Approach Hood with caution and respect, as this peak is not the right place to make a mistake or initiate a beginning ski mountaineer. The best way to get some experience on Mount Hood is to go above the ski area to the Palmer Glacier, but start skiing from below Crater Rock or the lower vents near the bottom of the Hogsback.

A view of the upper Old Crater route (left) and the Hogsback/Pearly Gates route (right). Note the large bergshrund crevasse blocking the path up the mountain.

Left: Mount Hood from near the Timberline Lodge.

Illumination Rock

Dr. Jon's Recommendations

The easiest way to access Mount Hood is from the south side at Timberline Lodge a few miles off of US Highway 26. From here the standard "Pearly Gates" and "Old Crater" routes are directly climbed up the Palmer Glacier from the Timberline Resort.

◆◆/◆ **Old Crater Route** Two separate couloirs can be found from the summit ridge dropping directly south into the Old Crater. In a good snow year, you can easily ski the west ridge directly from the summit, then choose one of the two narrow couloirs that can be 50 degrees for the initial 150 feet of the ski. If you are able to wait until 9:00 or 10:00 a.m. in May or June, after a sunrise ascent, the snow will have softened and the conditions into the crater will be ideal. Once near the sulfur vents, choose to either head skier's left to the Hogsback and down to Timberline Lodge via Palmer Glacier, or a steeper variation to the west of Crater Rock to Palmer Glacier is also possible. This route is a 4–8 hour climb up for a vertical mile (5,280 feet), and a 30 to 90 minute ski descent.

◆◆/◆ **Pearly Gates to Hogsback** More direct, steeper, and narrower than the Old Crater. If you are very skilled you can probably ski around or even jump over or off the bergshrund that guards the Hogsback depending on the time of year and conditions. Be aware of steam vents, which are hazards on both sides of the Hogsback, as you ski southwest then south down toward Palmer Glacier and Timberline Lodge.

◆■ **Palmer Glacier** A nice wide-open glade below the Hogsback and Crater Rock; you can ski down to Timberline Resort and back to Timberline Trailhead on groomed ski runs.

◆◆/◆ **Wy'east Face** This ski line is great once you can navigate the cliffs and small chute coming from the end of the southeast ridge, as Sylvain Saudin did in 1971. In a good snow year, the drop-in point is up to 60 degrees, but doable with some technical jump turns. Below the initial steepness, the sweeping face has lots of room and decreases in angle the further down you ski—from 45 degrees down to 30 degrees or less. Exit to your parked vehicle at the Mount Hood Meadows Ski Area near treeline.

◆◆/◆ **Cooper Spur** Steep, steep, steep. This is probably the most classic line on Mount Hood. It is east-facing, and drops almost directly from the summit or very abruptly from the short southeastern ridgeline of Hood. A fall higher up could be fatal, but the skiing is so pure, especially in April, May, or June when the face gets some strong morning sunshine. Ski with a partner and enjoy this one for a 4-mile run and a vertical mile of descent! Cooper Spur takes you east initially, then northeast lower down as you descend below 8,600'. Find your way back to Tilly Jane Campground for the Cooper Spur Trailhead. Cooper Spur can be a great intermediate ■ ski descent if you decide to climb about halfway up the Spur for 3,000 vertical feet before it gets too steep.

Dr Jon's Extra Credit: Three additional ski lines off the summit to the northeast, north, and northwest, respectively, include the **Snow Dome, Sunshine,** and the **northwest ridge.** You could ski to the vicinity of **Sandy Glacier** off the northwest ridge and explore some ice caves as well. Many routes, including **Cathedral Ridge** and **Yocum Ridge,** can be accessed from Sandy Glacier. **Leuthold Couloir** and **Reid Glacier Headwall** are also steeper but rewarding lines. Enjoy your ski adventures off the summit of Hood in less-traveled areas but always study maps of the area, use common sense, and carry proper gear on your new explorations.

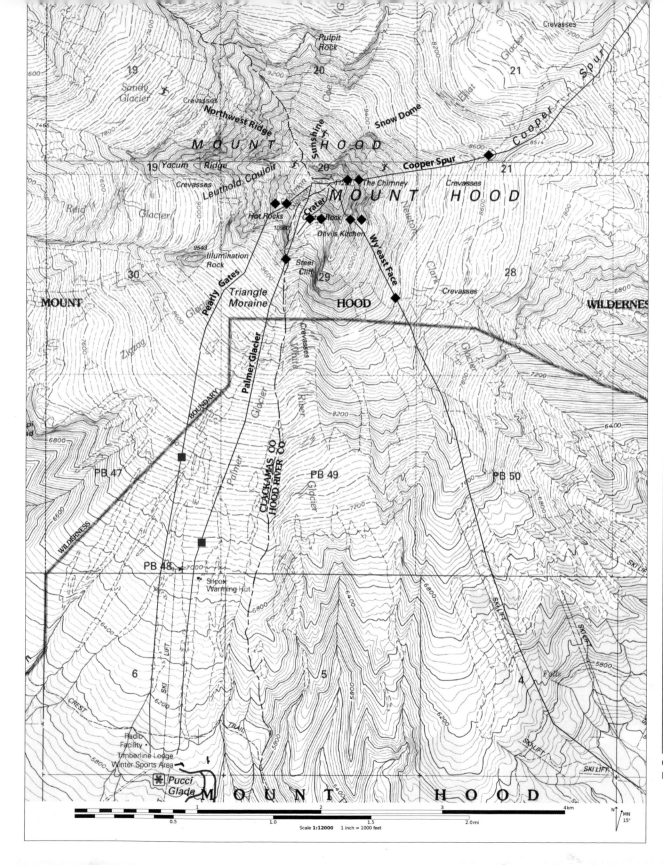

Chris Davenport drops into the Cooper Spur Mother's Day 2012.
Photo By Ted Mahon

Mount Jefferson

Isolated Seekseekqua

10,497 ft | 3,199 m
(44° 40′ 27″ N; 121° 47′58″ W)
Ski Descent May 21, 2014
First Ascent Ray L. Farmer and
E.C. Cross, August 12, 1888
First Ski Descent Unknown

The adventure starts in the forest, while camping near the terminus of the Milk Glacier and snowfield before the climb.

Following Hunt's Creek Trail near Pamelia Lake to access Milk Creek and the PCT.

Failure in Isolation Only

After skiing St. Helens with Mike Lewis, (see chapter 4) I arrived at the Pamelia Lake Trailhead on the afternoon of May 20 on a clear, sunny, warm day in north-central Oregon. I had a lot of energy and thoughts of spending the night on the very top of Mount Jefferson, the second highest volcano and peak in Oregon. It was a long drive from the Portland Metro area and took longer than I thought to get going on the trail. At a starting elevation of only 2,500 feet, you are hiking through a true Oregonian temperate rain forest when you start slogging to the steep southwest side of Jefferson toward Pamelia Lake. This was my lowest elevation trailhead start of any peak so far. As the afternoon wore on, I was already feeling like there wasn't going to be a chance to get up to the top of Jefferson for a bivy camp and the sunrise. Traveling north on the Pacific Crest Trail, I crossed a deep gully, a clearing, and Milk Creek before continuing farther up the trail in some thick woods. After another hour had passed and I was still slogging through the woods, I hit snow at about 5,500 feet. "At some point I have to turn east to find the west rib route on this peak," I told myself. I left the trail and headed east into the woods. Jefferson was fogged in for the afternoon, so after another half hour I had no idea where I was headed. Suddenly my intuition took over. "Go back down the trail to the river and from there you can access the west side of the mountain."

Realizing I had failed, I headed downhill, back to the PCT, and eventually back out to the Milk Creek crossing. I pushed up the drainage and made a camp along the river at about 4,700 feet. It would be nearly 6,000 vertical feet of climbing the next morning. As the sun began to go down, the skies cleared, and the mighty Mount Jefferson showed its face to the east. It was looming, and I had that nervous feeling I always get before I set foot on a peak that I have never climbed or skied. I downed some ramen noodles and a dehydrated lasagna meal, brushed my teeth, and was soon asleep, eager to get through the night and take on the challenge.

I awoke before dawn to the rumbling sound of the stream. Even though I wasn't sleeping on the summit, my camp here was spectacular. Jefferson resembled a Himalayan giant from this angle and I also reminded myself that sometimes it's not about sleeping on a summit, it's about so much more. Leaving my overnight gear in

The sun was very warm near the summit after climbing in cold shade conditions most of the morning.

Walking along the ridge to explore the different ski lines to make the best decision about the descent.

Looking north you can pick out Hood clearly, and Adams and Rainier if you look more closely on the horizon.

A nice look at the lower west slopes of Jefferson, which begin softening to corn conditions in May around 9:00 or 10:00 a.m.

the tent, I took only snacks and a liter of water and was on my way, climbing a narrow avalanche gully of Milk Creek in the alpenglow. Nearly a month's worth of climbing and skiing peaks allowed me to move very efficiently. In the frozen crust of the gully I took a quick break when the angle steepened near the base of Milk Glacier (snowfield) and I put on my crampons. It was just me and the mountain as I gained the start of the west rib, which was almost 2 miles long.

The rising sun to the other side of Jefferson kept things cold, but there was no wind so conditions were perfect. The west rib is a narrow and steep ridge. I kicked my own steps in the ridge, which was a fun climb alternating between easy walking and steep pitches of snow. On either side of me were steep bowls and gullies in all directions. Most of the time it was best to stay on the ridge crest directly, and at times drop to the north of the ridgeline to climb steep snow slopes and small inset couloirs. The entire rib rises nearly 1 vertical mile (5,000 feet). The summit was getting closer and closer and all the while I got to scout a number of amazing lines to ski along this west aspect.

Around 9:30 a.m., after almost 5 hours of strong climbing, I was basically looking up at the final summit pinnacle. It was a short pitch of steep snow and ice, up to maybe 80 degrees for a short 15-foot section to gain the pinnacle. After careful inspection I deemed that it might just be possible to ski this peak directly from the top. I carefully climbed with my ice axe and kicked some clean steps into the steepest part.

After overcoming a few steps of pretty hard ice, I gained the pinnacle and was steps from the top. The summit was very small and crystallized in ice. Wow, dropping off the top directly would be a tough proposition.

A Quiet Volcano Worthy of a Presidential Name

Mount Jefferson was seen by Lewis and Clark in 1806, and because their expedition was supported by President Thomas Jefferson at the time, the explorers named it Mount Jefferson. Jefferson is a true monarch, towering over a mile above the surrounding landscapes. It boasts five glaciers, and the andesite-dacite stratovolcano can now be considered dormant because its most recent eruption was a small one around the year 950 AD with only a small cinder cone formation. In fact, Jefferson is considered the only major Cascade volcano without a major eruption for the past 10,000 years. Scientists are fairly certain that this basaltic lava and tephra formation within the cone will likely stay very quiet in the coming centuries compared to neighboring Mounts Hood or St. Helens. On a clear morning, which I was treated to that day, I was able to see St. Helens, Hood, Adams, and even Rainier to the north, while to the south were the Three Sisters, Broken Top, Bachelor, and Thielsen, as well as Diamond Peak. It felt amazing to be on such a large volcano, and the majority of the peaks I was looking at I had successfully skied from.

The lower reaches of the west face of Jefferson boast unlimited ski potential on your descent.

Ski Descents and Potential Ski Lines

If you are seeking solitude and a monumental ski challenge, Jefferson is your peak. Mount Jefferson is nowhere near as popular to ski as many of the other volcanoes in the state of Oregon. Mounts Bachelor and Hood see most of the state's skiers and are easy to reach. For Jefferson, the low elevation of the trailheads and more difficult accessibility, as well as the large amount of elevation gain, all factor into this volcano being isolated. Skiers willing to pack it in and go the extra mile, putting in the extra effort, will find that Jefferson can be one of the best volcanoes in all of the Cascades to ski, and one of the most rewarding. On that day in mid-May, I was able to ski off the summit and carefully drop down into the south Milk Creek gully where spring corn conditions awaited. The amount of vertical I went down felt like it went on forever!

Once you enter the "Gargantuan Couloir", there's no turning back; you are fully committed to a vertical mile of skiing!

The author at 10,000' in the mouth of the "Gargantuan Couloir."

Dr. Jon's Recommendations

The best way to access Mount Jefferson is from the west side at the Pamelia Lake Trailhead a few miles off Oregon Highway 22. The Milk Creek and ridge routes of the west, southwest, and southern aspects of the mountain are the shortest and most direct from the trailhead. Longer approaches to the north and east sides of Jefferson for the Whitewater Glacier and Jefferson Park definitely require effort and multiple nights. You can access these routes from the Whitewater Trailhead off Oregon Highway 22 as well. The best months to ski Jefferson are generally late April until the end of June. The earlier in spring you go, the better your chances are to ski up to 6,500 vertical feet and 13 miles round-trip.

◆◆/◆ **West Rib/Milk Creek Gullies** The safest way to climb the west aspect of Jefferson is to follow the west rib. Skiing the series of small faces and ridgelines is possible on the rib, but coming directly off the summit, the southern gully ("Gargantuan Couloir") is easiest to immediately access to skier's left (southwest). The gully is never steeper than 45 degrees, except if you are skiing right off the summit pinnacle. The southern gully starts narrow but broadens about 800 to 1,000 feet below the summit. Here it is possible to traverse farther south and enjoy broad and very long corn slopes of the southwest face and southwest ridge as you make your way down to the remnants of Milk Glacier and into the deep lower Milk Creek gully. A similar gully is to the north (skier's right of the west rib and after leaving the summit pinnacle), which is more bowl-shaped but

will also take you to the base of the west rib and into the deep lower Milk Creek gully. Exit back to your vehicle via the PCT and Pamelia Lake.

◆■ **Southwest Ridge/South Ridge** Skiing off these ridges offers a safer alternative to the west rib. From the red saddle just below the summit pinnacle, a nice gradual ridge takes you to treeline. Skier's right follows the southwest ridge into the trees and back to the PCT, and you get great views of the west gullies from this route. The south ridge variates from treeline and will take you to Shale Lake and the PCT at just below 6,000 feet. When climbing, access these two ski lines from Pamelia Lake. Once reaching the PCT near Milk Creek, you can follow the PCT southeast toward Shale Lake to choose either ridge.

◆■ **Jefferson Park Glacier** This ski line is superb in May when all of the crevasses and bergshrunds of the upper glacier are covered. After navigating on your skis to the northwest around the northern tower, which is part of the main summit pinnacle, the broad saddle of the glacier's highest point allows you to choose any number of lines down the glacier. Enjoy the long northwest ski run all the way back to your camp at Jefferson Park. In April you may be able to ski all the way back to Scout Lake.

An alternative is the steep and narrow couloir ◆◆ to the east of the northern pinnacle tower. In early spring, plenty of snow makes this line a classic for a few hundred feet until you get onto the glacier itself.

◆■ **Whitewater Glacier** The broad eastern flank of the entire volcano, Whitewater Glacier is the largest glacier on Mount Jefferson. Once getting off of the summit pinnacle, the first prominent notch and short col get you right onto the northeastern portion of the glacier. In April and May the skiing is crevasse-free and never exceeds 40 degrees, getting less steep as you descend. If you traverse to skier's left you can follow the glacier north and find yourself back toward Jefferson Park in no time.

Dr Jon's Extra Credit: Russell Glacier is yet another ski line you can seek out. Rather than dropping onto the Jefferson Park Glacier, you can traverse farther to the northwest and around a tower that separates the sources of the Jefferson Park and Russell Glaciers. Also off the south ridge is the southeast-facing **Waldo Glacier** that has some ski potential, but beware that this glacier will leave you a long way from your vehicle if you parked at the Pamelia Lake Trailhead.

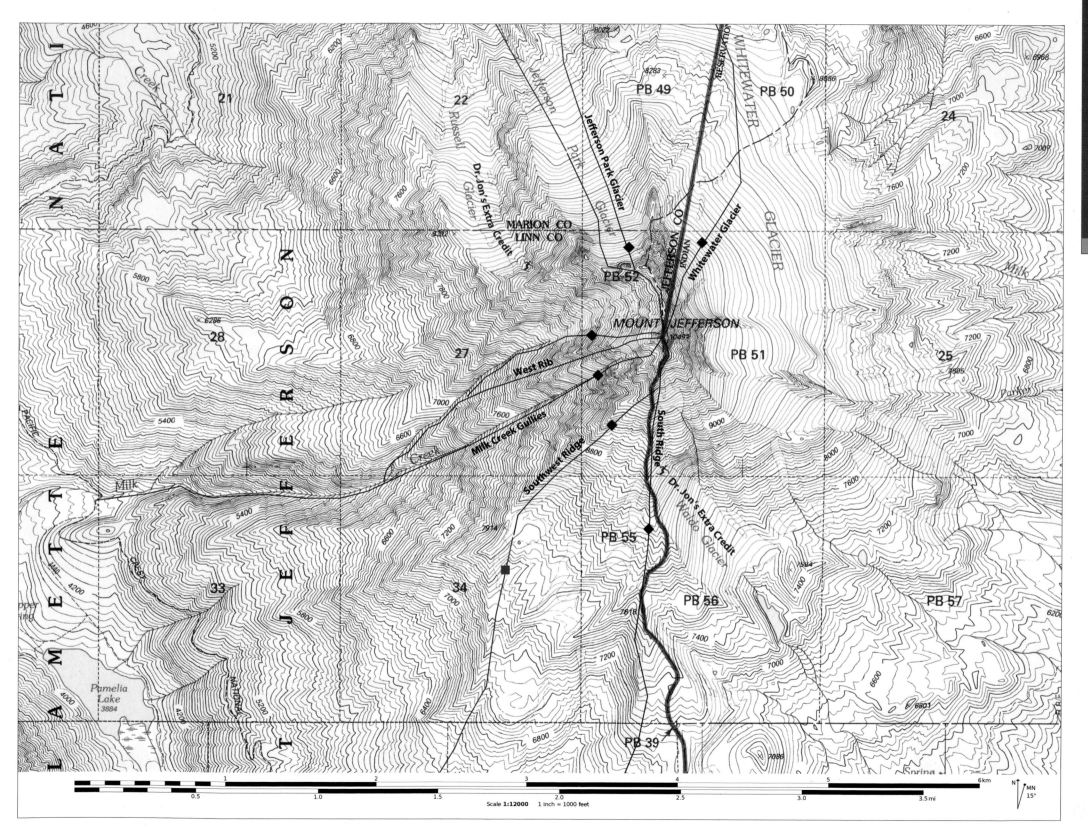

Scale 1:12000   1 inch = 1000 feet

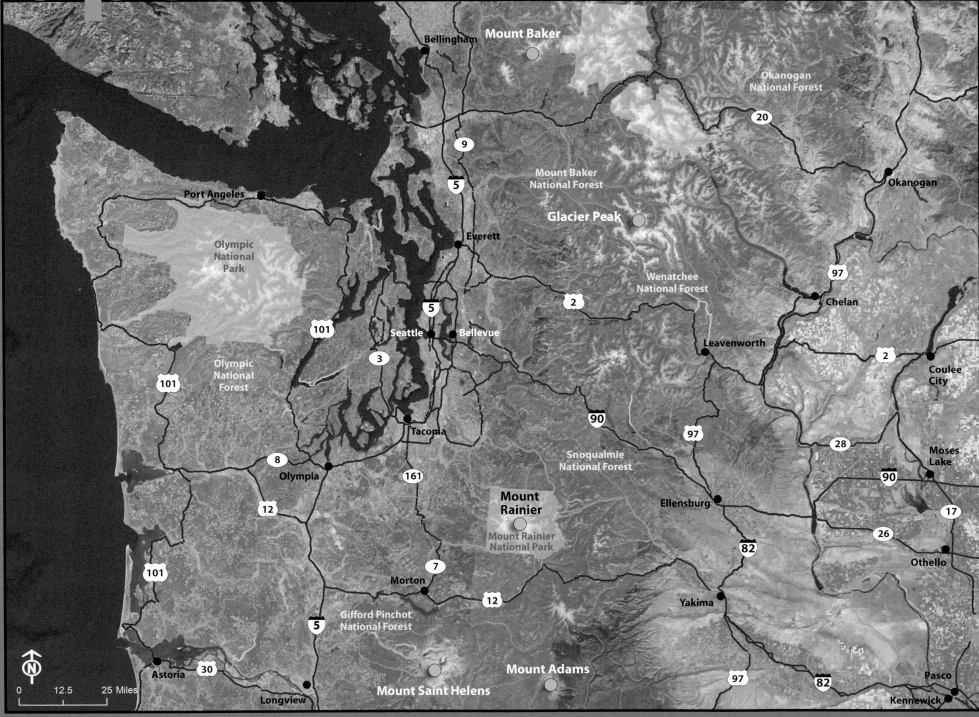

Mount Baker

Bellingham

Okanogan
National Forest

20

9

5

Port Angeles

Olympic
National
Park

Mount Baker
National Forest

Glacier Peak

Okanogan

Everett

Wenatchee
National Forest

97

Chelan

2

101

Seattle Bellevue

Olympic
National
Forest

Leavenworth

3

2

101

Coulee
City

Tacoma

90

28

Moses
Lake

97

8

Olympia

161

Snoqualmie
National Forest

Ellensburg

90

17

12

Mount
Rainier

26

Mount Rainier
National Park

82

Othello

7

Morton

Yakima

12

101

Gifford Pinchot
National Forest

5

Astoria

30

97

82

Pasco

N

0   12.5   25 Miles

Longview

Mount Saint Helens

Mount Adams

Kennewick

"The weather could not have been better and for a fair weather adventurer like myself that's perfect. I've got to admit it was very taxing following Jon up that hill. But I like that kind of thing. I had never before slept on the summit of a mountain. Growing up I could see Mount Baker from my parents' front yard, and looking up there now is gratifying in a way that is hard to describe." —IVAN LARSON

Above: Mount Rainier with Mount Adams in the distance.
Right: Mount Baker
Far right: Mount Saint Helens

Mount Saint Helens

Near Anniversary of the Eruption

8,365 ft | 2,550 m (46° 11′ 28″ N; 122° 11′40″ W)
Ski Descent May 19, 2014
First Ascent Thomas J. Dryer, 1853
First Ski Descent Hans-Otto Giese and Otto Strizek, 1930s
(ski ascent, likely skied down a bit as well); Fred Beckey skied from
the summit in 1961, this was the earliest recorded full ski descent.

Legendary Volcanic Peak

My confidence was very high when Mike and I began our
morning with the goal of skiing from the top of Mount St.
Helens. This would be the start of a new state of volcanoes,
but I was in familiar territory. All of the peaks in Washington
that I had remaining to climb and ski I had already visited
in recent years. Our slog began in the cold rain in the early
morning foggy hours of May 19. Departing to the Worm
Flows route at the Marble Mountain Snow Park Trailhead,
we pushed through a dense forest for the first hour and soon
the higher elevations gave way to deep gullies, a waterfall,
and sparse vegetation. Even though the mountain was fogged
in, we knew it was there waiting for us.

To ski from the crater rim of St. Helens is magical.

Approaching the slopes in a rugged and beautiful landscape.

Skinning up the peak, the morning became brighter and brighter. We burst out of the clouds and into abundant sunshine and blue skies. Looking to the southeast and east Mount Adams and Mount Hood poked above the sea of clouds like islands in the ocean. We saw the summit ridge above us, and soon made our way to the heavily corniced crater rim. With no wind and sunny skies, it turned out to be a perfect morning to stand on the top of St. Helens.

St. Helens is probably the most famous and recognized peak in the United States, even to my friends in other countries, many who refer to it as "that volcano that blew up." On May 18, 1980, the volcano blew its top, and when the dust finally settled, the peak had been reduced from 9,677 to 8,365 feet in elevation. Standing along the crater rim, Mike and I were in awe that thirty-four years ago one of the largest blasts in the history of the earth had taken place at this very spot, sending volcanic ash up into the earth's stratosphere and killing fifty-seven people. The plume of destruction was widespread. The pyroclastic blast was to the north and the plume extended to the west for dozens of miles. When the ash from the atmosphere came back down to earth, it was distributed clear across parts of the United States. Places like Billings, Montana, to the east, Denver, Colorado,

It's wise to stay clear of the cornice to avoid falling in! Mount Adams is visible to the east.

Mike Lewis putting in work to earn his turns. It's possible on the Worm Flows route to zig-zag your way to the crater rim without removing your skis.

and Omaha, Nebraska, even noticed volcanic ash deposited on car hoods and outdoor surfaces. Yakima, Washington, about 100 miles to the northeast, turned completely dark from thick ash in the air the day of the eruption.

New Landscapes Formed

As we transitioned on the summit from skinning to ski and board gear for our descent, we feasted our eyes down into the crater. Not only had two-thirds of a cubic mile of the volcano become displaced, but the inside of the crater has now formed a new glacier in the past thirty-plus years, called the Crater Glacier. Due to slope aspect, amount of shade, repeated avalanches into the crater rim, and high levels of snowfall each winter, this new glacier is up to 600 feet thick in some places, covering up to 0.4 square mile of land area. Geologically, this glacier in the crater rim of St. Helens is one of the youngest in the world, all because the volcano blew its top, changing the conditions of the mountain and now making the location favorable for the new glacier to be formed.

Climbing Permits Required!

When climbing Mount St. Helens, a permit is required from the Mount St. Helens Institute (MSHI) (**http://mshinstitute.org/ index.php/climbing/obtain_a_permit**). Permits cost $22 per person from April 1 to October 31. Permits are limited to 500 per day from April 1 to May 14, and 100 people from May 15 to October 31. The winter season runs November 1 to March 31, and permits are free.

New for 2015: Climbers will need to print their online permits at home and sign in at the trailhead climbing registers. Recyclable plastic permit holders will be available at the climbing registers to display climbing permits. Climbing permits must be carried at all times and displayed in a visible manner by each person while climbing Mount St. Helens.

Full climbing details are on the Mount Saint Helens National Volcanic Monument website: **http://www.fs.usda.gov/ detail/mountsthelens/home/?cid=stelprdb5145230**

The reason I did not spend the night on this summit was because the Mount St. Helens National Volcanic Monument prohibits overnight camping above 4,800 feet. Please abide by

Right: Mike Lewis enjoying the half pipe and waterfalls that the glacial troughs offer on the lower portions of the Worm Flows route.

Far right: Camping as high as possible in 2007 to enjoy an early morning ski.

The upper thousand feet of St. Helens is the ideal setting to enjoy gentle turns and corn snow in April, May, and June.

all NVM rules and regulations on your visit to St. Helens. You must sign in and sign out at either climber's registers located at the Climber's Bivouac Trailhead or Marble Mountain Snow Park Trailhead before and after your climb and ski.

Ski Descents and Potential Ski Lines

Due to the recent volcanic activity and the continual threat of earthquakes and small eruptions in the crater, it is against the law to venture into the crater of Mount St. Helens. I'll admit, there are probably tons of awesome steep ski lines into the crater, but the risk of cornices giving way to avalanches and the dangers of volcanic activity inside the crater are very real so please stay out of there and follow the law! Only the southwestern, southern, and southeastern aspects allow climbers and skiers to take advantage of the relatively gentle ski terrain that St. Helens offers to ski mountaineers. It is possible by way of the easiest routes to skin directly to the summit and crater rim of the peak, which can be an incredible experience with unbelievable views and history to ponder along the way.

Dr. Jon's Recommendations

◆■ **Worm Flows** The Marble Mountain Snow Park Trailhead at 2,700 feet is usually open year round. Just below the summit a brilliant wide-open snow slope of soft corn awaits for nearly 4,000 feet down to timberline. After the first 2,000 feet, there are a series of minor gullies you can navigate. Volcanic rock ribs separate gullies getting to timberline and to the Swift Glacier, so make sure you pay careful attention to where the trail is and where you need to exit into the trees in order to get back to the trailhead at the Marble Mountain Snow Park. At times the landscape looks the same, and people have become disoriented. From the summit you are generally skiing south and slightly southeast. Worm Flows is generally an excellent ski all the way back to your vehicle at the trailhead from December to March and in some years early April. May and June often bring excellent conditions above treeline, but expect to hike through the forest with your skis on your back first. This route is 12 miles round-trip with a 5,500-foot vertical ski descent.

◆■ **Monitor Ridge** By late April this trailhead generally opens at Climbers Bivouac, give or take a few weeks, depending on the season. Monitor Ridge is very similar to Worm Flows with less elevation gain to the summit and a shorter hike through the woods. Unless you are seeking a steep gully or bowl on either side of the ridge, none of the slopes you ski down to treeline ever really exceed 35 degrees. This route is excellent for a beginning ski mountaineer to explore a volcano! In winter, approach the route by skinning up the snowed-in road at the Cougar Snow Park at 2,200 feet, making a full climb and ski of nearly 6,000 vertical feet and 9 miles round-trip.

Dr Jon's Extra Credit: There is a trail that circles the entire mountain on St. Helens, similar to that of the Wonderland Trail around Rainier but much shorter. In the months of January through March, when snow coverage is high even at lower elevations, skiing around the peak and camping could be a true wilderness experience. Two additional routes, **Crescent Ridge** and **Butte Camp,** will also get you off the beaten path and you might just have the west ridge of St. Helens (Crescent Ridge) from Sheep Canyon Road all to yourself. Butte Camp is merely an alternative to the Monitor Ridge route, but this route starts from only 3,100 feet on the road west of the Climbers Bivy turnoff, heading north to the Butte Camp dome and then climbing north and northeast to the high point on the crater rim.

NATIONAL FORES

MOUNT ST HELENS

The Breach

MOUNT ST HELENS

LAVA DOME

1980 Crater

Dr. Jon's Extra Credit

Dr. Jon's Extra Credit

Monitor Ridge

Worm Flows

VOLCANIC MONUME

Swift Creek Flow

to Marble Mountain Snowpark

to Climber's Bivouac

Monitor Ridge

Worm Flows

Scale **1:12000**   1 inch = 1000 feet

N MN 16°

1   2   3   4km

0.5   1.0   1.5   2.0 mi

Mount Adams

A Return of St. Elmo's Fire

12,276 ft | 3,742 m (46° 12′ 09″ N; 121° 29′27″ W)
Ski Descent May 22, 2014
Bivy August 8–9, 2014
First Ascent A.G. Aiken, Edward J. Allen, and Andrew J. Burge, 1854
First Ski Descent Hans-Otto Giese, Hans Grage, Sandy Lyons, Walter Mosauer, and Otto Strizek, July 16, 1932

Sunset with no wind on the summit.

The north side of Adams provides a true wilderness experience, with dramatic views of Rainier to the north.

Instability Despite Success

After climbing Mount Jefferson in Oregon, as it was my final Oregon volcano, I returned to Washington to continue skiing the summits. Adams would be my seventeenth volcano skied in twenty-two days. I was a bit fatigued after the month I had endured, but I was also motivated to get to some of the biggest peaks of the project. I took advantage of a seemingly good weather day and willed my way to the top of the Adams stratovolcano for the sixth time in my climbing career.

The forecast for the day was supposed to be sunny with only a few high cumulous clouds. The midday heat was excessive as I strapped on skins and made my way up through the flats and mushy snow of the lower part of the mountain. When I reached treeline I could see the clouds building. All the signs of instability in the atmosphere were present: warm afternoon temps, light winds, and updraft. The puffy clouds also dropped some hail on me for short stints once I got above 8,000 feet. This was a clear indication that further updraft was happening. While I wasn't about to quit, I continued to climb toward Pikers Peak with a feeling that the

Cumulus clouds can build quickly into dangerous cells with warm afternoon temperatures, updraft, and mountains that are tall enough to stop their movement.

sky could open up any minute and that the clouds coming from the west were getting larger and darker with every second that came and went. My hope was that the storms were fast moving and would pass over quickly. For a short time I had to pack my skis on my backpack and boot hike up to the crest of the ridge.

When I reached Pikers Peak at 11,600 feet and took my skis off to continue skinning, the skis felt hot from the electricity in the air and my ice axe nearly burned my hand a bit as well. "I'll just push to the summit and see what happens," I told myself. "This is the Pacific Northwest in May, there's never lightning this time of the year." For the final 400 feet and fifteen minutes up the broad south face to the summit, I once again put my skis on my pack to finish and make the top. In intermittent fog and hail I took my pack off upon arriving on the summit. My skis were now buzzing from the electrical charges, and when I stuck them in the snow to de-skin, they were hot as well. "Yikes, this just doesn't feel right," I thought to myself. Just then the final straw that sent me packing and down on my skis to escape was the eerily familiar crash-flash-boom right in front of my eyes—and through me most likely. While I didn't get knocked out, the brightness of the flash pierced my eyes and ears and I felt the heat on my face. "I gotta get outta here!" I shouted out loud, even though I was all alone.

I honestly couldn't fathom being in this familiar place again. It was similar to the lightning incident I had when I camped on Mount Harvard in Colorado in 2011. I didn't think about the fact that I couldn't stay on the summit, I just wanted to leave. But the lightning had happened, so I immediately pulled off my skins and shoved them in my pocket in the midst of more cracking and popping in the air. All I could do was click in my skis and get down FAST!

Almost as soon as the lightning flashed again I was already down a couple thousand feet to the "Lunch Counter" area of Adams and I watched the storm pass over. Then, by 6:30 p.m., the sun came out and I decided I was too far down to make it back up to the top in a dramatically calmer and clear evening. (Although by 8:00 p.m., clouds and more hail and rain moved in so the summit would have been a wash anyway.)

After the storm cleared the mountain still beckons.

In hindsight, it was the perfect recipe for disaster. But it still doesn't answer my question: Why didn't I get killed? Luck, I guess. Maybe the current from the lightning went through all the metal (skis, poles, ice axe, etc.,) and not through me. Maybe I was conducting electricity but the charges at the top of the mountain weren't as strong as usual. I'm not sure of the answer but I am glad I came out okay once again. What a humbling experience.

Because the summer road for the South Climb Trailhead was closed 5 miles before the summer trailhead, I had not only slogged up the south side of the peak for 8,000 vertical feet but I was able to ski 7,500 feet for a spectacular and big day, nonetheless.

Summer Return for a Summit Bivy

As it turned out, I got the last laugh on Adams. In August, on a night with clear, calm, and warm summer conditions, I was joined by my friends Aaron, Tara, and Misha for an evening to remember on the top of Adams. Adams boasts the largest and flattest summit dome out of all the peaks in the Pacific Northwest, nearly a mile across and about a half mile wide. The sunset and full moon atop this huge crater made for one of the most impressive bivys of this project.

The tent was pitched on snow next to the emerging roof of what was at one time the highest fire lookout in the country. The lookout was staffed for four summers from 1921 to 1924. Then in 1929, Dean Wade and the Glacier Mining Company owned a claim and obtained sulfur at the summit from 1923 to 1936, employing 168 mule pack trains each year. Right: Sunrise

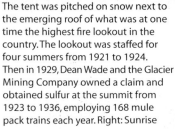

Mount Adams may be the second highest volcano in Washington, but the volcano as a whole has more volume than Mount Rainier. Adams is composed of several overlapping cones that form an 18-mile diameter base elongated on a north-south axis, covering an area of 250 square miles and a volume of 85 cubic miles. Adams also has twelve active glaciers that surround its summit, including the Cascades' second largest by volume, Adams Glacier, which is located on the northwest flank of the mountain. While the most significant Adams eruption

was roughly 4,000 years ago when the Aiken Lava Beds were formed, there are some active vents near the summit crater and Adams is considered a potentially active but dormant stratovolcano. The standard route to the top by way of the "South Climb" and parts of Suksdorf Ridge crosses only permanent snowfields, and provides the easiest route to the top.

Climbing Permits Required!

The Trout Lake Ranger Station is open during summer months to accommodate hikers and overnight campers within the Mount Adams Wilderness Area. Permits can be obtained at the ranger station. In the summer months, June 1 through September 30, a climbing permit (needed to venture above 7,000 feet) is required. The fee for a Cascades Volcano Pass for Adams is $15, but only $10 for weekdays Monday through Thursday. The most popular skiing on Adams is actually in April and May, so if the ranger station is not open, there is a self-registration permit system in place for the fall, winter, and spring months. Also be aware that the Yakima Nation controls the eastern side of Adams; traveling on the reservation is by permission only. Check local regulations before planning your trip. If you choose to ski Mount Adams between December 1 and March 31, a Sno-Park Pass is required at trailheads, and from April 1 through November 31 you must display a Northwest Forest Pass on the dash of your vehicle at trailheads. Link: **http://www.fs.usda.gov/detail/giffordpinchot/ passes-permits/ recreation/?cid=fsbdev3_005104**

Approaching the "lunch counters" camp site. The snowfields on the South Climb routes are skiable into July and August most years.

Left: North Cleaver and North Face Ski lines offer lots of skiable options.

Christy Mahon skis perfect corn on the 4,000 vertical foot Southwest Face of Mount Adams, May 2012. Photo by Ted Mahon

Ski Descents and Potential Ski Lines

Adams is an outstanding ski-mountaineering destination. The best and most skiable terrain keeps you clear of glaciers, and the non-technical nature of the peak combines relatively easy access with long and high skiable vertical distance, making this volcano a must-visit mountain. Classic lines off the south aspect of the mountain are very long and straightforward, accessed by South Climb Trail #183 and/or Forest Road 8040500 depending on the time of year, while northern routes on Adams can be steeper and more difficult. There is something here for everyone.

Dr. Jon's Recommendations

◆ ■ **Southwest Chutes** The ultra-classic quintessential ski line on Mount Adams. This line could very well be considered the number one ski line in all of the Pacific Northwest and in this entire book. There aren't many places on earth where you can ski up to a mile vertical on a single face and 7,000 vertical feet for your entire ski run. If you were to combine the South Climb Access Forest Road 8040500 (Cold Springs) with this entire line from the summit of the volcano, and in the correct time of year (January–March), it is quite possible to ski a bit over 10,000 vertical feet in one day on Adams. From the summit, head south and then drop to the west of Pikers Peak and you will be well on your way to a classic 35-degree ski line and one of the best ski descents of your life. (Nearly 7,000 feet vertical ski descent and 14 miles round-trip from the South Climb Trailhead.)

◆ ■ **Pikers Peak South to Aiken Lava Beds** From the summit, stay and travel near **Suksdorfs Ridge**, ski the broad south face of Adams below Pikers Peak into the vicinity of the Lunch Counters, and then enjoy volcanic rock and treed glades and minor chutes until arriving onto the flatter terrain of the Aiken Lava Beds directly south of the Lunch Counters at about the 6,000-foot level. In recent years, forest fires have thinned out the trees and the gentle terrain is an excellent place to cruise on Gotchen Glacier en route to your vehicle at the Smith Butte Sno-Park on NF-82, about 6 miles north/northeast of Trout Lake, Washington (up to 20 miles and 8,000 feet vertical).

◆◆ / ◆ **North Cleaver Ridge** and **North Face Routes** In 1854 the first recorded ascent of the mountain was by the North Cleaver. This ridge itself is a classic, and there are many options from the summit to ski. Direct descent of the sometimes narrow and exposed ridge is possible, but the north-facing cirque, headwall, and faces just to the west of the ridge are not only steep and skiable, but are an outstanding way to vary your descent from the top of Adams. Use Killen Creek Trail #113 and the Killen Creek Trailhead to access the north side of Adams. From Trout Lake, Washington, take Mount Adams Road for 1.3 miles. Continue on Forest Road 23 toward Randle for approximately 23 miles. Then take Forest Road 2329 (toward Takhlakh Lake) and follow it for about 5.3 miles to the trailhead. The Killen Creek Trail runs for about 3 miles until reaching 6,000 feet and intersects with the Highline Creek Trail #10 and the Pacific Crest Trail #2000. Round-trips typically range from 15–18 miles and 7,500 feet of ski descent.

Dr Jon's Extra Credit: There is a trail that circles the entire mountain on Adams and it can be used in late May to July to access ski routes on all sides of the mountain with an overnight backpacking trip. The PCT #2000 also passes through to the west of the mountain, so access to Adams is relatively easy. The **Northwest Ridge** and **Adams Glacier** is a challenging ascent and may also be a difficult descent depending on ski lines chosen and how crevassed Adams Glacier is. The **North Face of the Northwest Ridge** is a worthy objective. In addition, the steep "**Stormy Monday Couloir**" accesses **Adams Glacier** as well and provides a steep and narrow but fun ski. All north-side options on the mountain require an overnight backpack, excellent ski-mountaineering skills, and an adventure mentality. To access **Adams Glacier** directly, follow the Adams Creek Trail #112 southwest from the trailhead along Forest Road 2329, and you'll reach the base of the glacier above 7,000 feet. Other places to explore on Adams include **Lava Glacier and Ridge,** as well as **White Salmon Glacier**, also known as "**Avalanche Glacier**" as this was the site of the largest debris and ice and snow avalanche in the Cascades in recent years (1997).

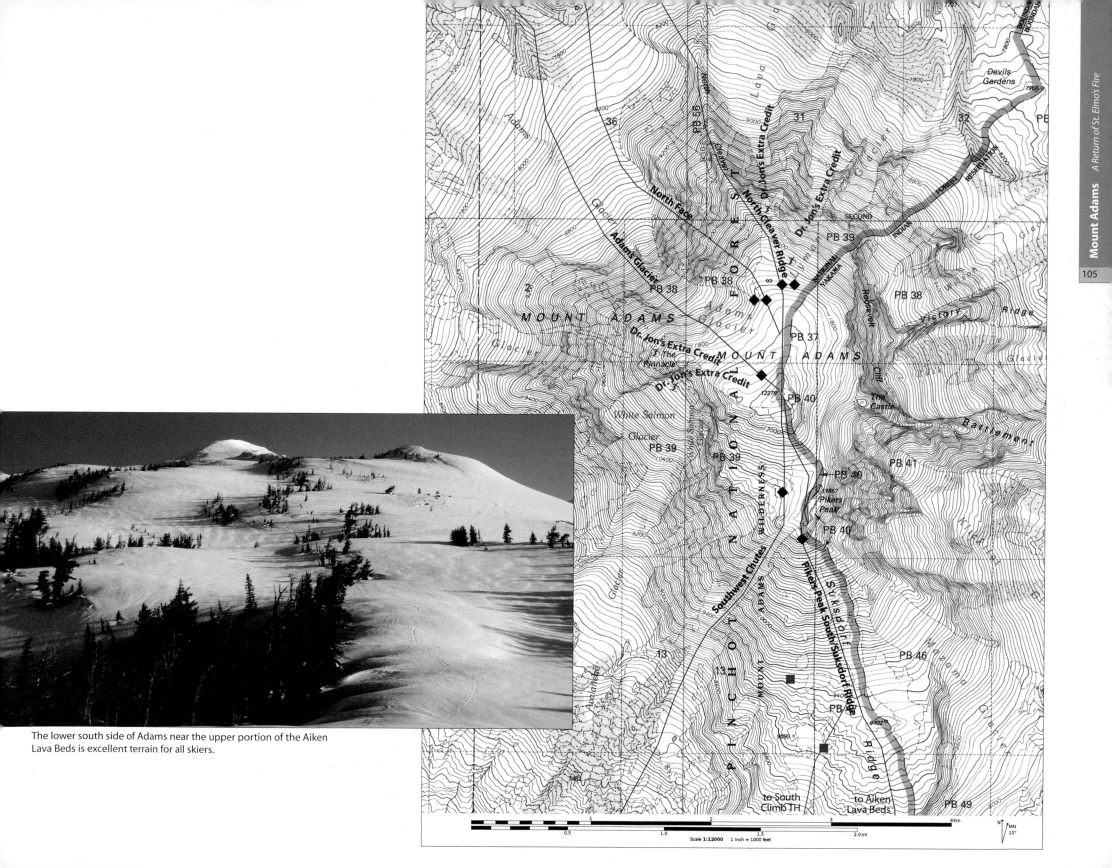

The lower south side of Adams near the upper portion of the Aiken Lava Beds is excellent terrain for all skiers.

Devils Gardens

36   31   32

North Face

Adams Glacier

North Cleaver Ridge

Dr. Jon's Extra Credit

PB 56

PB 39

PB 38   PB 38

MOUNT ADAMS

Dr. Jon's Extra Credit

The Pinnacle

Dr. Jon's Extra Credit

MOUNT ADAMS

PB 37

PB 40

White Salmon Glacier

PB 39

PB 39

The Castle

PB 41

PB 40

Pikers Peak

PB 40

WILDERNESS

Southwest Chutes

Suksdorf

Pikers Peak South / Suksdorf Ridge

PB 46

PB

13

13

MOUNT ADAMS

GIFFORD PINCHOT NATIONAL

9090

Ridge

to South Climb TH

to Aiken Lava Beds

PB 49

Scale 1:12000   1 inch = 1000 feet

0.5   1.0   1.5   2.0 mi

1   2   3   4 km

MN 15°

Mount Rainier

The Mountain Tacoma

14,411 ft | 4,392 m (46° 51′ 10″ N; 121° 45′ 37″ W)
Bivy August 10–11, 2011
Ski Descent May 24, 2014, several others 2010–2015
First Ascent Hazard Stevens and Philemon B. Van Trump, 1870
First Ski Descent Dave Roberts, Kermit Bengston, Charles Welsh, and Cliff Schmidtke, July 18, 1948

High Camp on the Ingraham Flats at 11,300′.

Opposite: Tahoma Glacier on the west side of the mountain offers solitude and reflection.

Right: Liberty ridge (center), first skied by Chris Landry in 1980, offers a technical challenge and a 7,500-foot vertical climb that the author completed in a single push in 2010.

Looking down at 14,000', only steps from the summit of Liberty Cap, the steep snow and ice of Liberty Ridge tests the most seasoned mountaineers.

Mountaineering Icon of the Lower Forty-Eight

The Mountain was like an old trusted friend. Out of all the volcanoes I had skied for this project, I was looking most forward to skiing Mount Rainier again. The crowning icon of the Cascades and the northwest United States, Mount Rainier is Washington's highest peak. The massive volcano is the most popular climbing destination in the Lower Forty-Eight contiguous United States, and the signature of Mount Rainier National Park. People from all walks of life come to Mount Rainier National Park to explore its beauty, and serious mountaineers use the peak as a training tool for other mountains on other continents. Since 2008, I had not only climbed Rainier from several routes, but I had skied the peak, and also used it for preparing to climb and ski in other parts of the world on many of the international expeditions I have been on. It's very true that if you can handle the weather, glaciers, and crevasses on Mount Rainier, you can generally handle conditions on most mountains of the world.

A Big Nostalgic Day on a Big Mountain

Returning in the dark morning hours of the 24th of May, I began my very long summit journey from the parking lot at Paradise just as I had done many times before. I was joined by my good friend Chris who flew in the day before, and we were excited to tackle the peak together. I reflected on so many memories of this special place as we skinned up to treeline and in the dark found our way onto the slopes of the Muir Snowfield at first light. Some of the pressure was off to actually spend the night on the top of Rainier, as I had already successfully done that in 2011, but combining a one-day push of the peak for 9,000 vertical feet and also get a ski descent done was a big task—one I was ready for. Slogging in the dark and into the magical hour light, my mind wandered through all of the amazing memories, climbs, and experiences that Mount Rainier had blessed me with through my twenty-plus ascents and multiple ski descents of the peak. Entire books have been written about Mount Rainier, and I felt as if my own personal history with the peak was no different. In fact, my PhD dissertation focused on Mount Rainier, yet it would still be hard to do the mountain justice in any single book, let alone in a simple chapter in this story. Mount Rainier will always hold a special place in my mountaineering career, and will always challenge me to keep my backcountry skills sharpened to precision.

Basecamp near the Carbon Glacier below Liberty Ridge.

Climbers Perceptions and Permit System Management

As I climbed higher toward Camp Muir, I thought about the two summers I had spent on Mount Rainier working on my Doctoral Dissertation from 2008 to 2009, which I published in 2010. I got to know several members of the Climbing Ranger Team, which also allowed me to climb the mountain more than I had anticipated. More importantly, I handed out surveys to climbers that asked many questions across the demographic of up to 10,000 climbers annually that attempt to climb the mountain. The primary objective of my research on Mount Rainier was to develop new knowledge about the different demographic backgrounds, visitor experiences, and perceptions of inherent risks associated with a typical summit attempt on one of the icons of modern mountaineering. The goal of the project was to conduct a survey to measure the social and physical concerns of visitor use through a sample of Mount Rainier climbers. Data were collected during

Camp Muir is a busy place in the summer climbing season where climbing permit system management is a priority.

the high climbing season at each study site from climbers involved on the southeast (Muir basecamp) and northeast (Schurman basecamp) sides of the mountain for the two most frequented corridors to climbing routes on Rainier. The survey focused on identifying indicators that have a significant effect on the mountain climber's perception and visitor experience for climbing Mount Rainier. I essentially asked the question "Why do you climb?"

Basic applied significance further examined the most important and lasting conceptual framework of the National Park Service, known as "visitor carrying capacity." A clear understanding of the effects crowding has on the visitor experience and carrying capacity exists through past studies of backcountry encounter norms, and perceptions of visitors to the more popular areas of Mount Rainier National Park. According to my research, crowding does not appear to be a concern for Mount Rainier climbers, as three-fourths of climbers stated that the number of people they encountered was within an acceptable limit for them. Out of 340 respondents, 75% answered yes (n = 254), and 25% answered no (n = 86). By specifically isolating Mount Rainier climbers and adopting the Visitor Experience Resource and Protection Framework (VERP), conclusions were made through relevant primary indicators as to how the visitor experience of Mount Rainier climbers is perceived. Primary indicators for "optimal" experience on the mountain as reported by climbers were components of geophysical risks and hazards, reasons people climb, and concerns for the environment. Variables of concern (i.e. high winds, cold temperatures, climbing with friends/family, climbing for a challenge, human waste issues, trash issues, trail erosion) were deemed as indicators to impact an "optimal" experience for Mount Rainier climbers. Furthermore, results may assist the NPS as to how the high-use climbing corridors of Camps Muir and Schurman can be continually managed for future climbing seasons. In particular, permit system management fees also were evaluated, and in recent years the price of an annual climbing pass has been adjusted to meet the needs of ranger assistance to climbers in climbing corridors where more people are located. (For example, climbing pass prices were about $30 in 2008, increased to $43 by 2011, and were $45 in 2015.)

More solitude can be found away from standard climbing routes on Rainier.

Following in the Footsteps of History

As we arrived at Camp Muir just before dawn that morning, I was not only pleased at our pace, but I was ready to tackle the route of the first ascent of Mount Rainier from way back in 1870. At that moment it also dawned on me that it would also mark the first time in my career that I decided to go from the parking lot to the summit in one push, and I'll remind you, it's a pretty long way! Late May afforded us long days of almost 18 hours of daylight in the Pacific Northwest, which are a real treat. It starts to get light around 4:45 a.m., and even by 4:00 the peak lit up some as the horizon could be slightly seen.

Skiers navigate some crevasses on the ascent through the lower section of Mount Rainier's Fuhrer Finger, May 2012. Photo by Ted Mahon

An amazing Washington landscape before sunrise ascending above 13,000'.

We departed above Camp Muir around 5:00 a.m. in the growing light, but there was nothing much going on except a few climbers headed up the standard Disappointment Cleaver (DC) route. After a short break, a snack, and a switch from skis to crampons, we took a ridge leading above Camp Muir and ascended toward Gibraltar Rock. As we got higher, the views got better and better. Morning light is always my favorite. The snow slopes were firm and the route was in pretty good condition. Once the sun came up, the best light showed, and the real climbing began. Blue skies above fog were in store for the morning!

The crux of the Gib Ledges route is where the ledges narrow and where you meet the Gib Chute. Both looked good and felt solid so we continued upward. A steep snow pitch of 45 degrees or so helps you gain a little spot near the top of Gib Rock. Looking down to the south from here the views begin to get impressive and you realize just how far you have come.

Leaving Gib Rock, the angle lessened and a few minor crevasses were lurking, but we continued on safely for another hour or so up the dome (as I call it) toward the crater rim. We met up with a couple of guys near the summit as they wrapped around from the DC route. They looked a bit shocked to see us carrying skis. The late morning was brilliant: Rainier really came out with the sun, and there were abundant blue skies as we were above the clouds for a while. Walking through the crater rim to the upper side and the true summit is always a nice reward. Active vents can be seen here, and we were soon standing on the summit in calm light winds, warmed by the sunshine!

Volcanology, Crater Geology, and Glaciology

There are few places on earth with so many powerful earth processes taking place. As I stared into the crater and peered at the geothermal steam rising from some of the snow-free volcano walls, I remembered that Mount Rainier is considered an active stratovolcano. While there has not been significant eruptive activity from Rainier since the mid-1800s, the peak is considered a "Decade Volcano," classified by scientists as one of the top sixteen volcanoes in the world with the likelihood to erupt and cause the greatest loss of life and property. To this day, seismic swarms, which are small series of several earthquakes over a two- to three-day period, are measured in the vicinity of Mount Rainier's crater rim. The most active swarms consist of up to five earthquakes of roughly 3.0 magnitude recorded atop Mount Rainier. Each month several earthquakes also occur even during periods between the swarms.

Sunrise in the crater

Mountain Meteorology: Recalling a Dream on a Cold and Windy Night in the Crater

I stood on the true summit and peered down into the crater on a rare calm morning at over 14,000 feet. It had come full circle—it was that day in 2011 while camping in the summit crater of Rainier where my idea to climb and ski the twenty highest peaks in thirty days was born. "A goal without a plan is just a wish" is one of my favorite quotes that I live by. While I still had two more peaks to climb and ski and at least one more summit bivy on Baker, it was at this moment I felt that I finally had a chance to fully accomplish my goal of climbing and skiing the twenty peaks all within the month of May. My dream was becoming a reality. Planning, preparation, training, execution, and perseverance all came into play throughout my journey that actually began nearly three years earlier when I had nearly lost my tent in gale force winds at this very same spot on the crater rim. Once again, this month in the Pacific Northwest—as well as the two and a half years since I had spent the night

on all the 14ers in Colorado—had proven to me that anything is possible, you just have to be willing to sacrifice and give it your best.

It was only the second out of over twenty times that I had stood on the summit of Mount Rainier with no wind. Why is it usually so windy on the summit? The simple explanation is that Mount Rainier is so close to the Pacific Ocean and stands over 14,000 feet higher than the surrounding landscape. Storm fronts and prevailing winds slam into the peak from the west with a strong force for most of the year. Only in the months from about mid-May through September does consistent high pressure move on shore and into central Washington, providing some mornings of calm conditions. But climber beware, weather on Rainier is unpredictable. Cold fronts, low-pressure storm systems, and fog can move in very quickly, especially in the winter months. In the winter, days are shorter, weather windows are smaller, and your margin for error is less when trying to climb and ski Rainier. The best time in my opinion to ski the peak is in May or June.

Geothermal heat from the volcano keeps the areas of both crater rims free of snow and ice, and has formed the world's largest volcanic glacier cave network within the ice-filled crater with nearly 2 miles of passages and tunnels. A small lake, about 130 by 30 feet and 20 feet deep, occupies the lowest portion of the west crater beneath more than 100 feet of ice and is accessible only through the caves. The lake is the highest in North America with a surface elevation of 14,200 feet.

About 5,000 years ago Mount Rainier was actually higher. Geothermal activity, glacial erosion, and minor eruptions weakened the volcano to the point where a massive debris avalanche took place. The resultant lahar and massive debris flow of ice, water, mud, volcanic rocks, and snow—known as the Osceola Mudflow—removed up to 1,600 feet from the height of Rainier, depositing the massive debris flow all the way to the site of present day Tacoma, on Puget Sound, 30 miles away.

There are twenty-six active glaciers on Mount Rainier, covering 36 square miles of the volcano. Many of the glaciers are receding, carving out deep valleys and canyons on the flanks of the volcano. These glaciers were at their largest extent during the little ice age of the mid-1800s, but have since receded thousands of feet up the valleys on Mount Rainier. The most significant measuring stick for climate change in Washington and the Pacific Northwest is the Nisqually Glacier and the glacier bridge along Paradise Road in Mount Rainier National Park. In the early 1900s the extent of glacial ice reached the bridge, but now the Nisqually Glacier terminus is nearly a mile above the bridge and nearly out of sight around the valley corner.

Always a Dangerous Climb

In one of the worst disasters on the mountain in over thirty years, six climbers—two guides and four clients—last heard from on May 28, 2014, were presumed dead on May 31, 2014, when low-flying search helicopters pinged the signals from the avalanche beacons worn by the climbers. Officials concluded that there was no possible chance for survival after the climbers fell 3,300 feet while attempting or returning from the summit by the Liberty Ridge climbing route. Searchers found tents and clothing, along with rock and ice strewn across a debris field, on the Carbon Glacier at 9,500 feet, possible evidence of a slide or avalanche in the vicinity where the team went missing, though the exact cause of the accident is unknown. The bodies of three of the guest climbers were spotted on August 7, 2014, during a training flight and recovered on August 19, 2014. As of this writing, the bodies of the fourth guest climber and two guides have not yet been located (as first reported by *The Seattle Times*).

Upper left: The carbon glacier is the lowest elevation glacier in the contiguous United States, 3,500 feet at its terminus. Left: Chris Davenport, Jess McMillan, and Jim Morrison just below Mount Rainier's broad summit plateau, on a one-day climb and ski of the Fuhrer Finger. Photo by Ted Mahon

Climber descends the "boot pack" on the Muir/DC Route; a large trough is created by hundreds of climbers. The Muir Snowfield can be seen far below to the left. Right: Chris Davenport skiing just above the pinch of the Fuhrer Finger, May 2012. Photo by Ted Mahon

Climbing Permits Required!

In order to climb Mount Rainier, to climb above 10,000 feet, or onto any glaciers, an annual Mount Rainier Climbing Pass must be purchased. As of 2015, a climbing pass for the calendar year was $45 per person 25 years and older, and $32 per person for 24 years and younger. Climbers must also submit a reservation for a wilderness permit, obtain a climbing permit, and register upon arrival at Mount Rainier National Park to climb. All climbing pass and climbing permit information and registration details can be found here: **http://www. nps.gov/mora/planyourvisit climbing-pass.htm**.

Full details about climbing Mount Rainier, as well as frequently asked questions and how to get started on your trip and climbing route plan, can be found at **http://www.nps.gov/mora/planyourvisit/climbing.htm**.

Ski Descents and Potential Ski Lines

We clicked into our skis and descended. Skiing from the top of Mount Rainier is actually a pretty dangerous and challenging proposition. While there are more than thirty-five routes and even more variations that have been repeated as climbing routes to the top, there are about five consistently skied lines on Rainier that are reasonably safe and up to twenty-five lines overall that have been skied. There are many more ski-tour options below the summit, and in the coming years there will be many more bold ski mountaineers that commit to challenging lines on Rainer that have yet to be skied. Although the first ski descent from the summit was not done until 1948, many had skied to Camp Muir in the 1920s and the 1935 National Alpine Ski Championships were held on the flanks of Rainier. In the 1930s and '40s the infamous "Silver Skis" races were held annually as skiers sped down terrain from Camp Muir to Paradise.

The best way to access Mount Rainier in the winter months is by Paradise in Mount Rainier National Park. The road to Paradise is open year-round, but make sure your vehicle carries chains from November 1 to April 30. The second best access to Mount Rainier is at the White River Entrance on the east side of the park.

First light as skiers start up Mount Rainier from Paradise with the broken Nisqually Glacier dominating the view of the mountain. The Fuhrer Finger ski line is seen at center. Photo by Ted Mahon

Dr. Jon's Recommendations

The five safest ski routes on Mount Rainier are listed. Skiing in late April to June on Mount Rainier guarantees maximum snow coverage, longer days, minimal crevasses, and the safest weather conditions on the volcano.

◆◆/◆ **Fuhrer Finger** The ultra-classic and best ski line on all of Mount Rainier (first skied in 1993 by Don and Pete Pattison with Mike Hattrup). You can access the Finger from Paradise by climbing Nisqually Glacier. From the Summit Crater and Point Success, ski south and follow the western edge of the upper Nisqually Glacier. The Fuhrer Finger itself is a narrow couloir of snow between 11,700' and 9,700' and it connects the Nisqually Glacier up high to the Wilson Glacier below and to the south and west. The narrowest sections of the Fuhrer Finger are about 75 yards wide, but timing is everything. April, May, and early June provide the best skiing of the Finger, and the later in spring you go, the larger the crevasses get on the lower Nisqually Glacier. If you ski the line in March or April it is possible to get nearly 11,000 vertical feet by skiing all the way from the summit to Nisqually Bridge. Round-trip from Paradise is 14–15 miles depending on conditions.

◆ **Emmons/Winthrop Glacier** An aesthetic glacier route, with a more remote feel than the standard DC route. When filled in by heavy snowfall in late spring, this route is very safe, with minimal hazard from the many deeply buried crevasses. There is excellent skiing in the large bowl from 11,000–13,000 feet, where recent glacial conditions have created a consistent 30–35 degree slope in the area known as "The Corridor." From the true summit on the crater, ski down north toward the saddle between Liberty Cap and the summit crater. Upon reaching the saddle, angle down and to the east and then to the northeast. In March or April, the bergschrund that guards easy access to the saddle may be buried and skiing east and northeast onto the upper Emmons Glacier may be quite simple. By June or July, the Emmons will be riddled with many more crevasses, making this ski descent more difficult. On the way back to your vehicle, the trail below Glacier Basin (5,900 feet) is often unskiable after early spring, making a full round-trip from White River Trailhead 17 miles.

◆◆/◆ **Disappointment Cleaver (DC)/Ingraham Glacier/Cadaver Gap** This has been the standard route for climbing Mount Rainier for decades (16 miles round-trip from Paradise to the summit and back). Leave the southwest side of the summit crater, then angle to your southwest and down the Ingraham Glacier. This line will be skiable through Cadaver Gap to Ingraham direct in early season (March, April, May, and early June). Later in the year it will require hiking the talus slope through Cathedral Gap, followed by a difficult crossing of the broken-up Ingraham Glacier. By late June, the easiest descent route may require you to follow your boot pack down, and even down-climb the Cleaver.

◆◆ **Gibraltar Chute** This is the most direct route to the summit and back down. Climbing the Gib Ledges along the Cowlitz Cleaver is likely the best way to preview the line up close. This line is south facing, and steep! Later in the spring (June) the bergschrund around 10,500 feet might be a considerable issue when it is time to leave the chute, get off the glacier, and ski southwest over to the safety of the Muir Snowfield.

◆◆ **Tahoma Glacier** A west side Rainier volcano climb and ski route. Camping near St. Andrews Rock at 9,300 feet not only allows for summit attempts and a great line called the "Sickle," but ski tours on the lower glacier accessed by the Wonderland Trail and the Westside Road are great in March, April, and May. This is a multiple-day backpacking option (22–30 miles round-trip).

◆■ **Muir Snowfield** The classic day trip or overnight adventure in mid-winter (December–March) to Camp Muir at 10,200 feet. Leaving from Paradise you still get almost 5,000 vertical feet to ski, and the terrain ranges from steep chutes to moderate alpine glades. The Muir Snowfield itself, from 7,200-foot Pebble Creek to Camp Muir, can provide 3,000 skiable vertical feet year round.

Dr Jon's Extra Credit: While the most straightforward and frequented ski lines and objectives have been mentioned, Mount Rainier offers dozens of other ski lines and even more variations that have never been skied. Extremely difficult objectives include **Liberty Ridge/Carbon Glacier** (first skied by Chris Landry in 1980), **Ptarmigan Ridge, Mount Tahoma, Mowich Face, Wilson Headwall, Paradise Glacier, Kouts Glacier,** and **Van Trump Park.** The Interglacier is also a fine ski route alone, or when combined with skiing **Emmons Glacier** and using **Camp Schurman** from the White River entrance to the park. **Little Tahoma** (11,138 feet/3,395 m), an eastern satellite peak of Rainier, also has some ski potential off the south face that very few have skied. One could spend a lifetime exploring Mount Rainier National Park on skis!

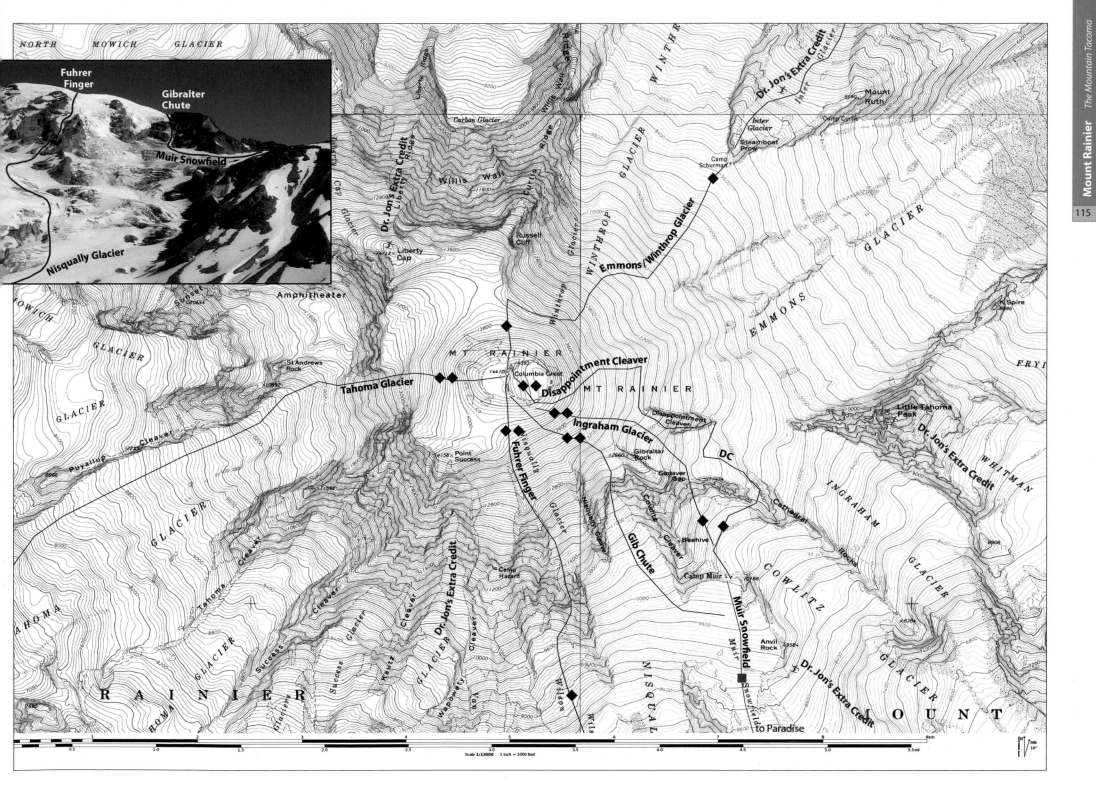

NORTH MOWICH GLACIER

Fuhrer Finger

Gibralter Chute

Muir Snowfield

Nisqually Glacier

Dr. Jon's Extra Credit

Dr. Jon's Extra Credit
Liberty Ridge

Carbon Glacier

Willis Wall

Russell Cliff

Liberty Cap

Amphitheater

WINTHROP GLACIER

Emmons/Winthrop Glacier

Camp Schurman

Inter Glacier

Steamboat Prow

Camp Curtis

Mount Ruth

EMMONS GLACIER

K Spire

MT RAINIER
Columbia Crest

Disappointment Cleaver

Tahoma Glacier
St Andrews Rock

MT RAINIER

Disappointment Cleaver

Little Tahoma Peak

Dr. Jon's Extra Credit
WHITMAN

Ingraham Glacier

DC

Gibraltar Rock

Cadaver Gap

Point Success

Nisqually Glacier
Fuhrer Finger

Cathedral Rocks

INGRAHAM GLACIER

Beehive

Gib Chute

Cowlitz Cleaver

Camp Muir

COWLITZ GLACIER

Camp Hazard

Muir Snowfield

Anvil Rock

Dr. Jon's Extra Credit

RAINIER

Tahoma Glacier

Success Cleaver

Kautz Cleaver

Wapowety Cleaver

Wilson

NISQUALLY

to Paradise

MOUNT

Scale 1:12000   1 inch = 1000 feet

Glacier Peak

White Mountain: The Icy Isolated One

10,541 ft | 3,219 m
(48° 06′ 45″ N; 121° 06′ 50″ W)

Ski Descent May 27, 2015
First Ascent Thomas Gerdine, 1898
First Ski Descent Sigurd Hall and
Dwight Watson, 1938

Crossing the Pacific Crest Trail near Red Pass before heading towards the White Chuck Glacier basin.

Darkness to Darkness—Dawn to Dusk Mission

This isolated giant was going to be an adventure. I was preparing myself for the longest day of my life by resting and catching up with my good friend Troy in Seattle the day before I would set out to climb and ski Glacier Peak. Glacier would be the farthest peak from the trailhead for the entire month, and the longest day yet, rivaling the day I skied all Three Sisters earlier in the month. On the morning of the 27th I drove from the comforts of Seattle and followed the highway to Darrington in the dark. By 4:00 a.m. it was already starting to get light and by the time I was off through the temperate rain forest in approach shoes with skis on my back, I barely needed a headlamp. I remembered my climb of Glacier Peak in the fall of 2010 from the same approach: the North Fork of the Sauk River. That year I started in the dark, and I finished in the dark for a total of 34 miles round-trip. That was mid-October, the days were shorter, and this time I had skis to hopefully speed my travel as well as my descent. I was hoping that I could make it to the top and back to my truck before dark, and was set to give it my best effort. It was my nineteenth peak in May, and yet I was as motivated as ever.

The forecast called for an approaching cold front off the Pacific and rain that would stay for two days starting that afternoon. It was now or never because all I had left to climb was Baker, and if this storm system socked in for a couple of days, I would only have time to attempt Baker once before the end of the month. I had no choice; I would push on no matter what. If I couldn't make the summit of Glacier, I wouldn't make my goal of twenty peaks in thirty days.

At timberline about 7 miles into the day, I reached the snow line. I skinned up to the ridge near the trail junction to the PCT (which was buried in snow), skirted a ridge between Red and White Passes, and took in some views above the timber at about 6,500 feet. It was only 8:00 a.m., but the clouds were already rolling in. As I descended into the White Chuck Glacier basin and toward the volcano, visibility dropped to zero. I followed my best sense of direction and continued to head northeast toward the peak. Sometimes the ridge leading to Disappointment Peak below the true summit was visible, and I would adjust my path along the border of White Chuck Glacier. I slogged on in silence. "I really hope my intuition is right on this one," I thought. As long as I could make the top and ski down in fog, I could always follow my tracks back. The morning wore on, but weather conditions were calm, and the incline increased. I felt like I was going the right way. I hoped for the best. Soon I had to put the skis on my back and set a boot pack. For several hundred yards I was headed up a steep 40-degree incline. The fog got thicker, but I knew where I was. A few moments of flat came and so did some slight clearing. The sun came out, and I could see I was on Disappointment Peak (9,755 feet), only a few hundred yards and less than 800 feet from the summit.

All fogged in on the summit.

Counting my steps and pushing as hard as I could, I finally topped out. The summit crater was flat, and it felt familiar to when I was there almost four years earlier. I couldn't see a thing in the fog but my altimeter read 10,600 feet. I had made it! It was 12:30 p.m., but my concern came with the oncoming storm system. I couldn't see anything, so I had no idea if I had time until it hit, or if I would just be fogged in for good and could just follow my tracks. After a few quick photos and a quick video, I swallowed an energy bar and transitioned onto my skis. I wasn't about to waste any time getting out of there. I was able to follow my boot tracks. I skied down to Disappointment Peak, off the steep pitch, and within minutes I was cruising along White Chuck Glacier toward the PCT and White Pass. The fog stayed above me in the basin, but then I had to climb back up to skirt White Mountain near the pass. As the afternoon wore on I was lucky, and as I skied from White Mountain and White Pass back to the trail and snow line, the skies cleared for a bit. Fortunately the storm never came until later in the afternoon, and by then I was only an hour from my vehicle. A fourteen-hour day, and I only had to hike for an hour in the rain back to my truck, making it just before dark. I'll take it . . . one peak to go!

Skiing over White Mountain is fun on the way to Glacier Peak.

The Shrinking Glaciers of Glacier

Glacier Peak currently has eleven significant glaciers along its slopes. The glaciers have retreated an average of 5,380 feet (over a mile in distance) since the mid-1700s. The 1940s and '50s actually showed a period of glacial advance or growth that culminated in 1978 due to colder summers and higher average seasonal snowfall, but since 1978 a major recession of the glaciers has been observed and measured. From 1979 to the present 2015, most of the eleven glaciers on the peak have retreated nearly 2,000 feet. Milk Lake Glacier, on the north side of the mountain, melted away completely in the 1990s. In addition, I witnessed significant evidence of this glacial retreat when I was utilizing topographic maps to navigate and climb Glacier Peak for the first time in October of 2010. A topographic map from the late 1980s marks the former extent of White Chuck Glacier in the basin. Recession in only thirty years was nearly a mile up the White Chuck basin.

1988 USGS topographic map. The "X" marks the extent of the glacial recession. The glacier shown in the 1988 map was gone.

October 2010: Looking south from the summit ridge of Glacier Peak.

Icy Isolated Stratovolcano and Nearby Hot Springs

Glacier Peak is the most remote and least visited of the five major Washington Cascade volcanoes. Besides Mount St. Helens, it also has the most recent and active eruptive history out of the volcanoes in Washington. Although now considered dormant, active central vent eruptions of Glacier Peak producing lahars, pyroclastic flows, and lava domes have been dated as recently as the 1700s and stretch back to 13,000 years ago. Volcanic activity is also linked to hot springs near the surface around the base of the volcano. In particular, the Kennedy Hot Springs along the banks of the White Chuck River to the west of Glacier Peak used to be a popular destination en route to climbing the peak prior to October of 2003. On October 21 and 22, 2003, a massive rain and flood event wiped out the Kennedy Hot Springs, including Trail 643 in the valley, the cabin at the springs, and the road below. Essentially the access to the springs and the northwest approach to Glacier Peak, including some bridges along the PCT, were completely destroyed and closed off. It's true the springs were lost forever, and hopefully someday the trail approach to Glacier Peak along White Chuck River will be rebuilt. Until then, the most practical approach is the one I took, by way of the North Fork of the Sauk River and the PCT to access the southwest (White Chuck Glacier) and west sides (Sitkum) of Glacier.

The summit dome of Glacier Peak holds snow year round.

October 2010: In only 30 years the White Chuck Glacier disappeared from this location.

Glacier Peak's south ridge can be skiable nearly all year long.

Ski Descents and Potential Ski Lines

Glacier Peak has been climbed by many but skied by fewer people than the other four major Washington volcanoes. There are more than a dozen reasonable climbing routes and even more variations that have been repeated as climbing routes to the top, and there are at least a dozen ski lines to be explored on Glacier. There are many ski-tour options to access and enjoy Glacier; a multi-day approach and utilizing a basecamp may allow you to ski more than one line on this majestic peak. In the coming years there will be many more bold ski mountaineers that commit to challenging lines on Glacier, or at least to variations on current lines that have yet to be skied. The best way to access Glacier Peak is by the North Fork of the Sauk River from Darrington. Trail 649 can be accessed from near the Sloan's Creek Campground on Forest Road 49, 6.4 miles east off of the Mountain Loop Highway where there is ample parking. If accessing Glacier from the east, the Buck Creek Pass approach by Trail 1513 is most practical, but the hike is very long (nearly 15 miles one way). The trailhead is located near Trinity, Washington, 24 miles from Lake Wenatchee along Chiwawa River Road 62. Either way you choose will lead you to the most rewarding wilderness experience in all of the Pacific Northwest!

Dr. Jon's Recommendations

The four most practical and safest ski routes on Glacier Peak are listed. Skiing in late April until the end of June on Glacier guarantees maximum snow coverage, longer days, minimal crevasses, and the safest weather conditions.

◆■ **White Chuck Glacier/Disappointment Peak, South Ridge** The safest and easiest ski line on all of Glacier Peak. Best time to ski the line is March until early June. From the summit, the southwest face of Glacier is an easy snow slope to the top of Disappointment Peak at 9,755 feet. Dropping off the top of Disappointment Peak, the angle is almost 40 degrees for a short time. Snow on the east side of the ridge covers the Gerdine Glacier and is also a variation of the route. Ski southwest into the White Chuck Glacier Basin and across the lower reaches of the White Chuck Glacier on easy slopes. Hike, skin, or climb out, then ski down to the North Fork of the Sauk River crossing near White Mountain and White Pass on the return. Your full round-trip adventure will cover 34 miles and up to 10,000 feet of vertical climbing and skiing.

◆■ **Sitkum Glacier** The best skiing is to the west of the summit for almost 1,000 feet leading west, to skier's right, almost to the northwest to Sitkum Spire. In March, April, or May the Sitkum Glacier will be crevasse-free, with a handful of variations down the west face and into White Chuck River Basin. Return to your vehicle via the North Fork of the Sauk River (PCT to Red Pass [6,500 feet] to Trail 649). Extra Credit: Climb over and ski White Chuck Cinder Cone (5,600 feet) on your return to the North Fork of the Sauk River. The cone is not far from the PCT and is easy to skin up for excellent views of Glacier Peak.

◆ **Chocolate Glacier** This is the largest glacier on Glacier Peak. From the summit, drop north then east, to skier's right, and find the best line down the center of the glacier. Some crevasses may be problematic at 750 to 1,000 feet below the summit. In early season, February through April, you may be able to ski the entire glacier into the Suiattle River basin. By May and June, a better option around the 7,000-foot level is to veer to skier's right and follow Streamline Ridge to timberline and down to the Suiattle River. Approach this route by way of Buck Creek Pass (Trail 1513) and the Suiattle River Trail 798.

◆◆/◆■ **Frostbite Ridge to Gamma Ridge**—North and northeast ridge route. From the summit follow the north ridge across to the "rabbit ears" north sub-summit of Glacier Peak. From the rabbit ears stay on the west side of the cleaver and ski north then northeast past North Guardian Rock down Frostbite Ridge. At about 9,500 feet you will encounter the Gamma Ridge cleaver and North Guardian Rock. Ski northeast, to skier's right, down relatively gentle ■ slopes and across the North Guardian Glacier, the lower portion of the Dusty Glacier, and eventually connecting to Gamma Ridge Trail 791 and the PCT near the Suiattle River. This is a remote alpine glacier ski that is classic with mountains in all directions!

Dr Jon's Extra Credit: ◆◆/◆ **Frostbite Ridge** and **Kennedy Glacier** are both classic ski lines and climbing routes to the summit. Skiing down variations of these two features to the north and northwest of the summit are fine ski objectives. Follow the PCT north for 2 miles from the east side of **Glacier Peak** near the **White Chuck River**. Leave the trail and head east up toward **Kennedy Glacier** before the PCT heads to **Fire Creek Pass**. The rest is up to you to explore on this northwest portion of Glacier.

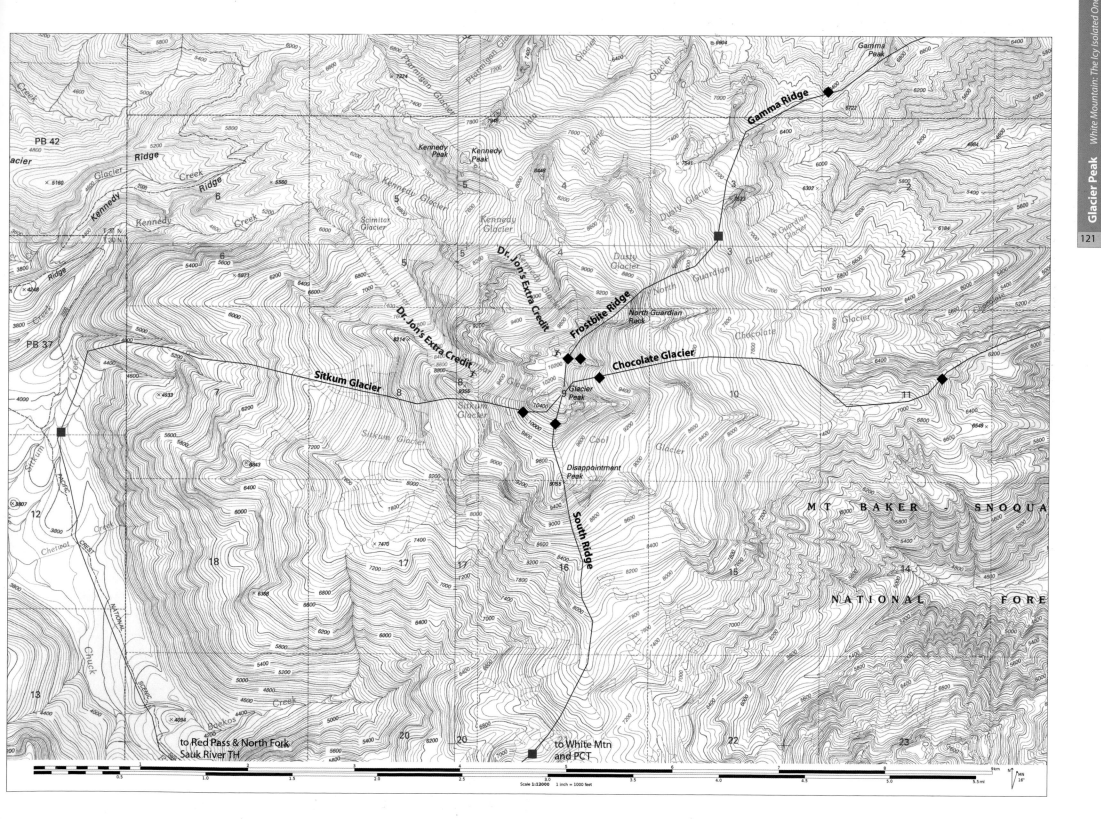

Gamma Peak

Gamma Ridge

Kennedy Peak

Kennedy Peak

Dr. Jon's Extra Credit

Dr. Jon's Extra Credit

Frostbite Ridge

North Guardian Rock

Chocolate Glacier

Sitkum Glacier

Glacier Peak

Disappointment Peak

South Ridge

MT BAKER - SNOQUA

NATIONAL FORE

PB 42

PB 37

Kennedy Ridge

Kennedy Creek Ridge

Scimitar Glacier

to Red Pass & North Fork
Sauk River TH

to White Mtn
and PCT

Scale 1:12000   1 inch = 1000 feet

Mount Baker

Koma Kulshan—Great Mount Carmel

10,781 ft | 3,286 m (48° 46' 38" N; 121° 48'48" W)
Bivy and Ski May 30–31, 2014
First Ascent Edmund Coleman, John Tennant, David Ogilvy,
Thomas Stratton, and Edward Eldridge, August 17, 1868
First Ski Descent Ed Loness and Robert Sperlin via Easton Glacier,
1930; Don Fraser and Hans-Otto Geise via Coleman Glacier, 1933

The sun going down on the final peak.

Meteorology My friend Ivan joined me for the climb and bivy of Baker. We ascended the original Coleman-Deming Glacier route. The Mount Baker Trail starts as a beautiful hike. We traveled through the forest to just below the hogback at 4,000 feet, then changed over to skis and began a spectacular skin up the glacier, then below the west faces of the Black Buttes and Colfax Peak. Mount Baker averages over 60 feet (720 inches) of snow per year, but there are areas nearby that get much more snow. The Mount Baker ski area to the northeast of the peak set a world record for seasonal snowfall in 1999 at 1,140 inches (95 feet!). Most of the fall, winter, and spring months (November through April and even into May) Baker gets hammered by storms coming off the Pacific and through the Strait of Juan De Fuca. This cold and moist air (influenced by frigid arctic air masses) slams into the prominent 10,781-foot volcano and drops more snow in some years than any other place on earth. Even in the summer, moisture from Puget Sound can drop snow on the higher reaches of the peak. By May and June, short high-pressure weather windows establish themselves on the peak (with longer periods of excellent weather in July and August), so when a weather window opens up, take advantage and ski the incredibly good conditions that persist on a warm sunny day. Since May is at the end of the winter season, the snow-pack is at its peak. To our benefit, there was so much consolidated seasonal snowfall on our route that a majority of the crevasses were filled in completely. Although we wore harnesses, roping up on the glacier was unnecessary due to the superb conditions.

20th Peak in 30 Days

It was time for the finale, the last summit to spend the night on and ski. The month of May was drawing to a close and I was excited to finish off my final peak on Mount Baker, one of the icons of the Pacific Northwest. I had only climbed Mount Baker one other time, in February 2011. I managed to summit via Easton Glacier on the south side in a whiteout, but hadn't been back since. I was determined to make this summit and ski of the peak memorable, and hopefully the views would be great, too.

The author taking in the views with Mt. Shuksan in the distance. Photo by Ivan Larson

Glacial Controversy

Hosting twelve active glaciers and 44 square miles of permanent ice and snow, Mount Baker has been mentioned more than once to have more glacial ice than Mount Rainier (which has 35 square miles of ice). Rainier, by comparison, has larger and thicker glaciers, so some have suggested Rainier still has more glaciated volume. Both mountains have had measurable glacial recession over the past century and are being closely studied with climate change and global warming implications (e.g., Easton Glacier and Nisqually Glacier). Nevertheless, the amount of glaciers and dangerous terrain on Baker is a concern to all who visit its rugged slopes and climb the mountain. Crevasses on Baker open up usually by mid-June through the end of the summer, so consider carrying a rope and other glacier travel gear on your adventures.

Summit of the Wounded White Sentinel

As 5:00 p.m. approached on the warm and windless afternoon, I crested the summit ridge above the Roman Headwall and skinned across the side of the Carmelo Crater rim to the highest spot toward the east, known as "Grant's Peak." A satisfying feeling overwhelmed me. "I did it, Twenty Peaks in Thirty Days!" I told myself. Not many people have been able to ski so many volcanoes and in such a short amount of time. Ivan reached the summit a few minutes after me and we exchanged high fives and got to work at establishing our camp. Sleeping on this summit for the night was a no brainer. The weather was so good and I had a few hours to relax, enjoy the views, set up camp, and savor the entire experience.

Looking down into the semi-active Sherman Crater, which emits toxic sulfuric gases.

"Wounded White Sentinel" is a term given to Baker because it is considered a reasonably active andesite stratovolcano that's covered in snow. Baker is one of the youngest of the major Cascade volcanoes. There are two craters near the summit. The Carmelo Crater is buried in snow along the broad summit dome while the Sherman Crater is on the south aspect and is the source of recent volcanic activity. In fact, while on the summit, the smell of sulfur coming from the deep Sherman Crater fumaroles was very nauseating.

The nineteenth century saw some of the most significant activity from Baker, but in the last fifty years, fumarolic activity, steam, smoke, and sulfuric ash as well as a ten-fold increase in heat emitted from Sherman Crater has led to Baker being monitored and heavily studied as an active volcano. Due to the heat, debris flows,

lahars, and snow avalanches have occurred and are possible on steep slopes near the crater rim. As recently as 2007, a significant avalanche and debris flow occurred on the Boulder Glacier of Mount Baker. Scientists continue to monitor the volcano, but suggest that the active nature of this Wounded White Sentinel won't turn pyroclastic like St. Helens did back in 1980.

Last Sunset on the Northernmost Bivy of My Goal

The tents were up on a leeward northern side of Grant's Peak. This was the first bivy of my career that I could look out and see the sun set over the ocean. As the sun went down I took plenty of time to reflect. I could see the Strait of Juan de Fuca off to the west, and I couldn't help but think about the moment in 1792 when George Vancouver and Joseph Baker got their first glimpse of this "very high conspicuous craggy mountain." The shiny water and red and orange colors of the sun setting gave this last summit of the ski portion of my project a brilliant exclamation point. To the north was Garibaldi in Canada, the northeast was Shuksan, to the east was Glacier volcano, to the south Mount Rainier, and to the southwest the Olympic Mountains. This was the northernmost bivy on the top of a mountain in my career, and one of the most rewarding—in late May the sun didn't set until almost 10:00 p.m., and then the lights from both the Seattle and Vancouver metro areas were brightly visible.

Decisions, decisions. Ivan Larson takes a break while we descend the Roman Headwall. Skiers and boarders can descend to the Easton or Deming Glacer (left), or the Coleman Glacier (right). Colfax Peak is at the center.

Ski Descents and Potential Ski Lines

It was a very short night. In the morning, first light came just before 4:00 a.m. By 5:00 a.m. the sun came up toward the northeast above Shuksan and cast some incredible light on the surrounding peaks and into the sky. I couldn't wait to ski down my twentieth and final volcano of the trip. Truth be told, there are at least six different quality routes and up to ten total ski routes on which to drop off this mighty volcano. With no wind, Ivan and I packed up in the warm morning sun, and ate our breakfast waiting for the snow to soften just a bit. For the last day of May, we were stoked to ski down one of the most spectacular peaks in the Pacific Northwest in perfect conditions. By 8:30 a.m. we clicked into skis and dropped off the highest point, retraced our tracks from the day before along Carmelo's Crater rim, and headed back over to the start of the Roman Headwall off of Baker's southwest aspect, as we would ski down the ridge and then down onto the Coleman Glacier. We had 6,000 vertical feet below us and nothing but smiles on our faces.

The author descends the Roman Headwall with a heavy pack, the Easton Glacier is far below.

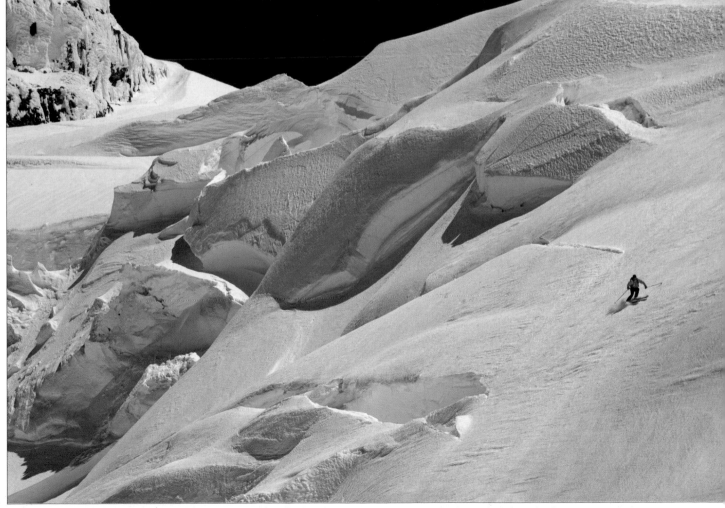

Chris Davenport flirts with the crevasses below the Roman Headwall on the Coleman-Deming Route, May 2012. Photo by Ted Mahon

The Coleman Glacier, with Baker (left), and Colfax Peak (right). Careful navigation to avoid cravasses is important.

The author skis on the Coleman-Deming Glacier with Colfax Peak above. Photo by Ivan Larson

Dr. Jon's Recommendations

Five of the best ski descents on Baker include:

◆ **Roman Headwall to Heliotrope Ridge** Drops off the southwest aspect, a classic 30–40-degee face, then meets the head of Coleman Glacier ■ at about 8,500 feet in the saddle between the Roman Headwall and Black Buttes, heading west back to the Mount Baker Trail. You can ski up to 7,000 vertical feet in 12 miles round-trip for this route.

◆◆ **North Ridge Options** Includes a complete ridge ski and variations back down to Coleman Glacier (the west-facing Coleman Headwall is an extreme ski descent choice as well). Roosevelt Glacier also skis to the northwest of the summit. Best skied in early season, March to early May, when Coleman's crevasses are covered.

■● **Easton Glacier South Slopes** Gentle Blue/Green slopes below the initial headwall (which is only 35 degrees) make for excellent sunny spring corn skiing. The Easton Glacier terminates at the Railroad Grade Trail, but in early spring (March) it's possible to ski almost 8,000 feet nearly back to your vehicle at the Park Butte Trailhead and 14 miles round-trip!

◆ **Boulder Glacier** You can drop directly off the true summit of Baker via Grant's Peak. Take an initial southeast set of your steepest turns off the summit, staying north of Sherman's Crater and Sherman's Peak for several hundred feet. Boulder Glacier then becomes less steep below 10,000 feet and you can ski up to 5,000 vertical feet down this glacier in March, April, and May, and a couple thousand feet farther once leaving the glacier. The Boulder Lake Trailhead is also nearly skiable back to your vehicle depending on the time of year.

◆◆ **Park Glacier** The longest ski route on the mountain, the initial headwall is very steep, up to 60 degrees, but the glacier that faces northwest to the east of the Cockscomb will allow you to follow the glacier (later at angles of 30–45 degrees) and then rolling slopes down 7,000 vertical feet from the summit, across the Rainbow Glacier, a traverse of the Sholes Glacier, down Ptarmigan Ridge, and back to the northeast to the vicinity of the Mount Baker ski area. If the Mount Baker ski area is not your desired destination, skiing down either the Rainbow Glacier and Rainbow Creek or the Park Glacier and Park Creek will take you to the basins to the east and southeast of Mount Baker and towards the northwest end of Baker Lake.

Dr Jon's Extra Credit: Extreme skiers might like to take on the challenge of the steep western face options off the top of the western summit dome, which drop down onto the most crevassed portions of the **Coleman Glacier** to the northwest. **Mount Shuksan**, a formidable peak over 9,000 feet high, is located within clear view of Baker. Explore the peak and give it a go if you haven't had enough fun on all these volcanoes already.

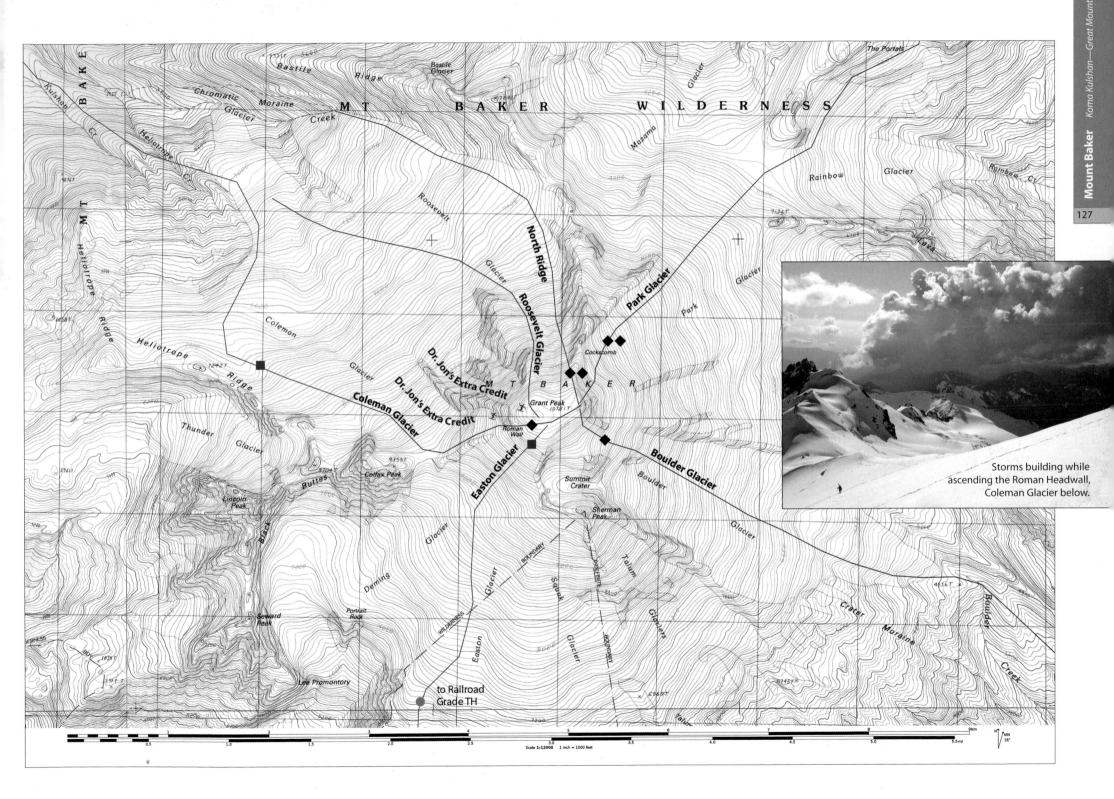

B A K E

MT

K U L S H A N

Kulshan Cr

Heliotrope Cr

MT

Heliotrope Ridge

Chromatic Glacier

Chromatic Moraine

Bastile Ridge

Bastile Glacier

Creek

M T   B A K E R   W I L D E R N E S S

Roosevelt

Mozama
Glacier

Glacier

The Portals

Rainbow   Glacier

Rainbow Cr

Lava

North Ridge

Roosevelt Glacier

Park Glacier

Park Glacier

Glacier

Coleman

Heliotrope Ridge

Glacier

Dr. Jon's Extra Credit

Dr. Jon's Extra Credit

Coleman Glacier

Cockscomb

M T   B A K E R

Grant Peak
10,781 T

Roman Wall

Easton Glacier

Thunder
Glacier

Black Buttes

Colfax Peak

Lincoln Peak

Seward Peak

Portrait Rock

Lee Promontory

Deming

Glacier

Summit
Crater

Sherman
Peak

Boulder

Boulder Glacier

Glacier

Glacier

Easton

Glacier

BOUNDARY

WILDERNESS

Talum

Sqak

BOUNDARY

Talum
Glaciers

Glacier

Crater
Moraine

Boulder
Creek

to Railroad
Grade TH

0.5   1.0   1.5   2.0   2.5   3.0   3.5   4.0   4.5   5.0   5.5 mi

1   2   3   4   5   6   7   8   9 km

Scale 1:12000   1 inch = 1000 feet

N
MN
16°

Storms building while
ascending the Roman Headwall,
Coleman Glacier below.

Sunset on Mount Hood. Photo by Mike Lewis

Afterword

The month of May 2014 for me will always be remembered as the time I skied the highest twenty volcanoes in the Pacific Northwest in thirty days. The journey of over 250 miles traveled by human power on the volcanoes and a bit more than 100,000 vertical feet skied in May was bittersweet when it ended. On May 31st, when I arrived back at the safety of the trailhead at the base of Mount Baker, I had taken my skis off for the last time for the project and it felt great. All good things have to come to an end, and although I felt ready to hang up my skis for the season, I had been on such a roll on the volcanoes that I couldn't believe it was all over. Projects for me in the mountains always amount to planning, hard work, adversity, perseverance, sacrifice, a slice of the unexpected, and of course, a finish line. I think even in our everyday lives if we pursue a goal, whether it's personal, professional, or even family-oriented, and if we plan well, execute, work hard, and overcome obstacles to get to where we are going, more often than not we will accomplish our goal. In the end for me it wasn't always about the summit, or actually getting to spend the night up there. "Twenty Peaks in Thirty Days" was about the journey, sometimes the suffering, and more importantly, I had so much fun doing it. Combining my passions of skiing with camping on the top of the highest volcanoes in the United States was amazing, and once again as my Chevy Tahoe cruised across the central Washington plains on my way back home to Colorado, I couldn't help but wonder, there are still so many more mountains to climb, so what am I going to get myself into next? Only time will tell. I can promise you that it will involve some degree of camping on a summit, clicking into a pair of skis, and making turns, while having the time of my life!

Appendix A: Dr. Jon's 2014 Chronology—*20 Peaks in 30 Days*, Cascade Volcano Log

Peaks Climbed, Skied, and Summit Bivouacs

Peak Name (Elevation in Feet)	Type of Volcano	Dates Climbed & Skied (2014)	Route(s) Climbed to Summit/ Ski Descent (● ■ ◆ ◆◆)	Round-Trip Distance (mi) & Vertical Feet Climbed/Skied
1 Mount Shasta, CA (14,179')*	Stratovolcano	W–Th, Apr 30–May 1	Avalanche Gulch ◆	11 mi – 7,300'
2 Lassen Peak, CA (10,457')*	Plug Dome	F–Sa, May 2–3	North Ridge / Northeast Face ◆	9 mi – 4,000'
3 Mount Tehama, CA (9,235')	Stratovolcano Remnant / Caldera	Sa, May 3	South Ridge / Southeast Face ◆/◆◆	12 mi – 2,535'
4 Mount McLoughlin, OR (9,495')	Stratovolcano	M, May 5	East Ridge / Southeast Face ■/◆	11 mi – 4,215'
5 Mount Scott, OR (8,938')*/X	Stratovolcano Remnant / Caldera	Tu, May 6 Bivy: Sa–Su, Sep 5–6, 2015	Ski: Crater Lake Rim Dr., Northeast Face Hike: Mt. Scott Trail ■/◆	· Ski: 30 mi – 3,500' Hike: 5 mi – 1,338'
6a Garfield Peak, OR (8,048')X **6b** Applegate Peak, OR (8,126')X	Crater Lake Rim Caldera	Tu, May 6	Rim Drive / South Face ● ■	6.5 mi – 1,750'
7 Mount Thielsen, OR (9,182')*	Stratovolcano	We–Th, May 7–8	West Ridge / Southwest Face ■/◆	10 mi – 3,700'
8 Diamond Peak, OR (8,744')	Shield	Su, May 11	West Ridge/ Southwest Face ■/◆	10 mi – 4,044'
9 Mount Bachelor, OR (9,065')*	Stratovolcano	Su–M, May 11–12	Northwest Ski Runs ■/◆	5.5 mi – 2,800'
10 South Sister, OR (10,358')*	Stratovolcano	M–Tu, May 12–13	Lewis Glacier, South Slopes / Prouty Glacier ◆	35 mi – 12,200' TSM
11 Middle Sister, OR (10,047')	Stratovolcano	M–Tu, May 12–13	Southeast Ridge / North Ridge ■/◆	35 mi – 12,200' TSM
12 North Sister, OR (10,085')	Stratovolcano	M–Tu, May 12–13	South Ridge / South Face ◆/◆◆	35 mi – 12,200' TSM
13 Broken Top, OR (9,175')	Caldera / Stratovolcano	Th, May 15	Nine O'Clock Couloir / North K & Eleven O'Clock Couloirs ◆◆	11 mi – 3,100'
14 Mount Hood, OR (11,239')*/**	Stratovolcano	F–Sa, May 16–17	Palmer Glacier / Old Crater Route ◆/◆◆	9 mi – 5,280'
15 Mount St. Helens, WA (8,365')**	Stratovolcano	M, May 19	Worm Flows, South Face ■/◆	12 mi – 5,665'
16 Mount Jefferson, OR (10,497')	Stratovolcano	W, May 21	West Ridge / Gargantuan Couloir ◆/◆◆	13mi – 6,500' PL 18mi – 7,800' TH
17 Mount Adams, WA (12,276') */**	Stratovolcano	Th, May 22 *Bivy: Sa–Su, Aug 9–10	South Climb, Pikers Peak / Southwest Chutes ◆	14 mi – 7,000'
18 Mount Rainier, WA (14,411')*/**	Stratovolcano	Sa, May 24 *Bivy: W–Th, Aug. 10–11, 2011	Gib Ledges, Cowlitz Cleaver/ Gib Chute ◆/◆◆ Muir/DC Route (Glaciers)	15 mi – 9,100'
19 Glacier Peak, WA (10,541')**	Stratovolcano	Tu, May 27	White Chuck Glacier, Disappointment Peak / South Ridge ■/◆	34 mi – 10,220'
20 Mount Baker, WA (10,781')*/**	Stratovolcano	F–Sa, May 30–31	Coleman – Deming Glacier / Roman Headwall, Heliotrope Ridge ■/◆	12 mi – 7,150'
TOTALS 20 Volcanoes Climbed	in CA, OR, WA	Skied 20 Peaks in 30 Days 10 Summit Bivy Nights		265mi – 100,859' (19.1 vertical miles)

Overnight Bivys on the summit are in bold
*Indicates overnight summit bivouac in addition to climbing and skiing the peak.
**Indicates peaks that were climbed and skied in years other than 2014 and on multiple ski routes in addition to the one listed.
X Indicates peaks climbed and skied but not summited, and not skied from the top due to bad weather. (Mt. Scott was summited in Sept. 2015 but not skied from the top in 2014).
TSM Indicates Three Sisters Marathon, the round-trip distance starting at the base of Mount Bachelor combining South, Middle, and North Sister including the May 12, 2014, summit bivy on South Sister.
PL Indicates round-trip distance and elevation for Mt. Jefferson from Pamelia Lake
TH Indicates round-trip distance and elevation for Mt. Jefferson from Pamelia Lake Trailhead, may not be skiable for start of the trail in the forest.

Congratulations to Dr. Jon on yet another amazing accomplishment: conquering 20 peaks in 30 days. *Skiing and Sleeping on the Summits: Cascade Volcanoes of the Pacific Northwest* demonstrates that *life is better outside;* a true testament to our motto, "Always in Charge." There seems to be nothing quite like the feeling of waking up on the top of a volcano, taking in the sunrise and skiing down.

—Team EnerPlex

Appendix B: Avalanche and Climbing Resources

Before you go, always check up on current weather, snowpack, avalanche conditions, and peak/route discussions. The following sites provide up to date information on these important parts of being aware in the backcountry:

Weather and Avalanche Conditions

AIARE The American Institute for Avalanche Research and Education | www.avtraining.org

American Avalanche Association www.avalanche.org

Current Mount Baker mountain route and weather conditions http://mtbakerclimbing.blogspot.com

Current Mount Rainier mountain route and weather conditions, as maintained by Park Service Climbing Rangers | http://mountrainierclimbing.blogspot.com

Mount Shasta Avalanche Center, Weather and General Climbing Information www.shastaavalanche.org

NOAA National Oceanic and Atmospheric Administration pinpoint weather forecasts www.noaa.gov

NWAC Northwest Avalanche Center Forecasts and Conditions for Oregon and Washington www.nwac.us

USGS Cascade Volcano Observatory http://volcanoes.usgs.gov/observatories/cvo/

Additional Helpful Climbing Websites, Forest Service and National Parks

www.cascadeclimbers.com Articles, blog, forums, trip reports and more from the entire Cascade range

www.wildsnow.com Colorado based, but includes excellent trip reports from the Cascade volcanoes from its contributors

Mountain-specific sites listed from south to north in the Cascade range

http://www.nps.gov/lavo/planyourvisit/hiking_lassen_peak.htm Lassen Peak and Lassen Volcanic National Monument

http://www.nps.gov/lavo/planyourvisit/hiking_brokeoff_mountain.htm Brokeoff Mountain in Lassen Volcanic National Monument

http://www.nps.gov/crla/index.htm Crater Lake National Park

http://www.fs.usda.gov Search Thielsen, McLoughlin, Three Sisters, Jefferson, Diamond.

http://www.fs.usda.gov/recarea/mthood/recarea/?recid=80001 Mount Hood Climbing Information and Permits

http://www.fs.usda.gov/mountsthelens Mount Saint Helens National Volcanic Monument

http://mshinstitute.org/index.php/climbing/ Mount St. Helens Institute, Climbing Permits

http://www.fs.usda.gov/detail/giffordpinchot/passes-permits/recreation/?cid=fsbdev3_005104 Mount Adams Climbing Passes and Regulations

http://www.nps.gov/mora/planyourvisit/climbing.htm Climbing Mount Rainier, Climbing Passes, Permits, and Planning your Climb.

http://www.fs.usda.gov/recarea/mbs/recarea/?recid=30317 Climbing Mount Baker Information

http://www.fs.usda.gov/recarea/okawen/recarea/?recid=79427 Glacier Peak Wilderness

Acknowledgments

I am so grateful to the tremendous amount of support I received before, during, and after I skied these awesome Cascade volcanoes in May of 2014. Amazing doesn't even scratch the surface when it comes to the people that have helped me make this book project a reality. First many thanks to my family and close friends. My Mom and Dad (Barb and Bob Kedrowski) for putting up with me all these years and letting me seek your advice during my many visits for dinner and out on hikes and around the house or on the golf course. Thanks to my brother Jared, his wife, Michelle, and my nephews Kash and Kaden. Also my sister Krista and brother-in-law Zack. This special ski journey is for you. My brother Robbe and his family: miss you guys. To my great friends Bob Pietrack, and his wife Lauren, as well as Chris Tomer and Leanne Cowell, you guys have been awesome in motivating me to continue this new N.O.D. story. Tomer, thanks again for your great forecasting outlooks when I did have decent cell coverage. Chris Davenport was so incredibly generous with his additions to this book and his inspiration for motivating me to pursue skiing volcanoes and taking Sleeping on the Summits to a whole new level. Ted Mahon, your photo additions are incredible, and I am so grateful for being able to use them to really show the beauty of skiing these giant volcanoes. To everyone who skied a volcano or spent the night on a summit with me: Mike Lewis, Ivan Larson, Misha Ramsey, Aaron Jenniges, Tony Sudekum, and of course the lovely Tara "Dactyl" Nichols. You guys were awesome to want to endure such suffering at the top of a peak all night and to reap the rewards of success and the magnificent sunrises and sunsets. To the Rainier clan, Chuck and Kathy Rowberg, Krista Shaefer, Steve Odegard, and Sonja Schaefer, thanks for allowing me to stay in your cabin near the park every summer on Rainier, and of course again when I came to ski. I have enjoyed our summits of Rainier together every bit as much as I did sleeping in the summit crater!

My editing and design team was fun to work with on this sequel, and without them this book could never be possible. Mira Perrizo edited the manuscript while Rebecca Finkel designed such a gorgeous journey. I am always grateful to work with you ladies. At the CMC Press, Sarah Gorecki oversaw the completion of the book and its publication, along with all the critical copy edits and finalizations. Sarah, I am so thankful for my new relationship with the CMC! To the Executive Director of the CMC, Scott Robson, and the board president, Kevin Duncan, thanks for believing in my abilities as a ski mountaineer and a writer. Special thanks to the Duncan family, including David and Kevin, both who are avid outdoorsman and skiers. I will always be grateful for our friendship, the partnership with Silver Oak, and the ability to take a fine bottle of Silver Oak to the summit of any mountain in the world, including these awesome Cascade volcanoes. John Fielder, thanks so much for motivating me to get my next book done and for mentoring my photography, and checking in on me from time to time on skis to make sure I am on the right track. To the Jenniges family—Aaron, Sarah, Jack, Remy, and Julia: I am so grateful for our friendship and your place to stay in the Portland/Vancouver area and a good meal anytime I pass through the Pacific Northwest. Sarah, what a generous addition to this book was your map expertise, and Aaron, thanks for your nutrition advice and ability to push me on this and other adventures. Troy Cunningham, thanks for keeping me company in Seattle in between the big peaks! To my sponsors: Silver Oak, Zeal Optics, Enerplex, Kastle Skis, Honey Stinger, Go Scope, Acli-mate, Mountain Hardwear, and the Vail Athletic Club: I am so appreciative of your support towards my goal on this project. There are so many more people I wish to thank that played a role in this new adventure: Vince Nethery, Ayn-Marie Hailicka, Zach Taylor, Kim Hess, Greg Tonagel, Todd Potestio, Connor Drumm, Jason Blevins, Avery Stonich, Jeff Morgan, Jennifer Broome, Natalie Tisdale, Patrick Jager, Jim Huckabay, Jillian Emery, Brandon Elley, Steve Swayze, Alison Levine, Christy Mahon, Justin Jacobs, Rafael Gutierrez, Minette Siegel, Ian Leggat, Lisa Martin, Dan Gillett, Jamie Starr and the crew at Dynafit/Salewa and many more that aren't named here. Thanks so much and always remember to enjoy the journey along the way, savor the views, and be on the lookout for *Sleeping on the Summits III* someday!